DOES THIS MEAN
MY KID'S
A GENIUS?

DOES THIS MEAN MY KID'S A GENIUS?

Linda Perigo Moore

63198

McGRAW-HILL BOOK COMPANY
NEW YORK   ST. LOUIS   SAN FRANCISCO
HAMBURG   MEXICO

1 2 3 4 5 6 7 8 9 F G F G 8 7 6 5 4 3 2 1

LIBRARY OF CONGRESS CATALOGING IN PUBLICATION DATA

Moore, Linda Perigo.
Does this mean my kid's a genius?
1. Gifted children—Education—Handbooks,
manuals, etc. I. Title.
LC3993.M66   371.95   81-3793
ISBN 0-07-042960-X   AACR2

Book design by Roberta Rezk.

For Steve, who doubled his share of
parenting while this book was in
production

Acknowledgment

The education of any child is a cooperative effort between parent and teacher. I wish to acknowledge those professional educators who have motivated, inspired and taught our GC.
Developmental Learning Center, Butler University, Indianapolis: Marge Fadely, Director. Charlene Gleaves, Salla Wilson, Pat Ober, Phil Kenneson (Science), Gloria Poore (Typing), Jeanne Kerstines (French), Claudia Nole (Spanish), Constance Little (Fiber Art), Peggy Cranfill (Drama), Dorothy Jeglum (Music).
Park-Tudor School, Indianapolis:
Jean Magel, Director, Lower School. Barbara Jester, Mary Ann Hurley, Judith Bruch, Michele Borgenhoff (French), Margaret Carroll (Library), Melanie Holmes (Music).
Meridian Studio, Carmel, Ind.:
Celana Roth (Piano).

Thank you.
L.P.M.

Contents

Preface

This book is not a recipe for gifted children. It is a guide for anyone with a child who is:

    a. more energetic   **c.** quicker than most
    b. more inquisitive   **d.** a bit of a mystery
                      e. all of the above

When we were told our son was gifted, we were overwhelmed by developmental concepts, professional jargon, educational decisions and emotional confusion. We suddenly had new responsibilities and new expectations—but we didn't quite know what they were.

> Who are gifted children?
> How smart is smart?
> Can anybody be one?
> What do we do now?
> Will it go away if we do nothing?

In 1971, the U.S. Department of Education categorized 2 million children as "Gifted and Talented." Today educators are saying there may be as many as 5 million. The increase has come about because of two significant factors:

    1. The functional definition of giftedness has been expanded. Rather than being limited to children with astonishing levels of academic ability and general intelligence, giftedness now in-

cludes those children with excellence in leadership skills, the visual and performing arts and (in some cases) athletics (Public Law 95-561).

2. In many school systems, the numerical plateau has been lowered to include IQ scores that range from 115 to 120. This has resulted in two specific groups of gifted and talented children: those with IQs from 115 to 160, and a smaller group with IQs of 160 and above.

Public school systems in almost every state are responding with increased programming to meet the special learning needs of these children. During the 1979–80 school year, forty states (acting under state statute) spent $117 million on gifted education. This involved the commitment of more than 12,000 teaching professionals.

And in keeping with the Gifted and Talented Children's Education Act of 1978, federal appropriations for gifted education (1980–81) will be an additional $6.28 million.

The public school system in America is an equalitarian structure. As gifted programs continue to evolve, almost every schoolchild (an estimated 45.7 million) will be scrutinized as a possible participant.

Millions of mimeographed notes will proudly announce the formation of "enrichment classes," "honors tracks" and "programming for exceptional learners." Hundreds of thousands of parents will suddenly become aware of heretofore undefinable criteria that can now affect their children. Most of these parents will not know what it means for a child to be labeled gifted and talented. Few will have experience with the evaluative tools used to select gifted children. Many will begin to wonder, "Is my child included?"

I am not an expert on gifted education. I am an expert on one gifted child and the interested observer of dozens more. I also happen to be an educator and intensely curious about the education and development of gifted children.

My mentor for this project was Marjorie Fadely, Director of The Developmental Learning Center of Butler University, Indianapolis.

To ease your reading, a couple of ground rules:

1. "GC" is used as an abbreviation for "gifted child." Because we say "GC" instead of "gifted child" when we read, I form its plural by adding an *s:* GCs.
2. To save us all of that he/she, his/her business, pronouns are used interchangeably. Sometimes a GC will be called "she," sometimes "he."

Each chapter is written with the following objectives:

- To remove the mystique that separates parents from educational decisions about their children.
- To humanize the stereotypic image of the gifted and talented child.
- To promote the concept that active parenting can enhance the giftedness of all children.

1

How Can You Tell?

Jennifer runs the Westlake Elementary third-grade class. A teacher is always present, but it is Jenny who tells the children what to do, when to laugh, how to construct the papier-mâché maps for geography and when it's all right to study quietly. Everybody knows she's in charge.

His teachers say that Charles never received attention as a boy. He was a quiet student, but a hard worker. When he was thirteen, while wearing a Boy Scout uniform, he forced his way into an apartment and with a camping hatchet attacked a teenaged tenant. One morning ten years later, he stopped to help a young mother whose car had stalled. He raped and murdered her. Then he drowned her three small children in the Ohio River. Psychiatrists say he had an IQ of at least 160.

Sean is enrolled in the applied mathematics program at Michigan State University. On October 31, he missed the regular meeting of the study group he helped organize. It was Halloween, and most fourteen-year-olds still like to go trick-or-treating.

Sarah's parents knew from the beginning there was something different about her. She sat up, walked and talked at much earlier stages than did her two sisters. At age five, she taught herself to read; but she was not a particularly good student. In fact, she had to take remedial math even to get into the state university. She's now a professor of law and a candidate for Superior Court Judge.

John is a C student at North High School, so his classmates were surprised when he earned a full scholarship to study at the Sorbonne in Paris. They didn't realize that John fluently speaks seven languages and two Chinese dialects.

Everyone knows about Larry's talent. As a high school student, he electrified his small Indiana community with athletic skill that challenged belief. No one was surprised when he turned pro.

WHO ARE THEY AND HOW CAN YOU TELL?

They've always been around. In prehistoric times they may have been the only people to survive. The Chinese, as early as 2200 B.C., had developed a civil service screening method that gave all positions of authority and responsibility to them. Plato thought they should be taken from their parents as early as possible and reared in a pure and sterile academic environment before taking their rightful places as governors. After Russia initiated the space race, they once again became popular in this country. Millions of dollars were invested in high school chemistry, physics and mathematics laboratories throughout the United States. The "College Bowl" was put on TV.

They have been called precocious, able, bright, eggheads, high achievers and exceptional learners. In the recent past, they were called genius. Today it's in fashion to call them gifted children.

GCs have been denied, denounced, fantasized and feared. But they have yet to be accurately defined. Just when you feel you could pick one out in a crowd, you come upon some strange incongruities. If he were a child today, Einstein probably would be placed in the school's "multicategorical resource room" for slow learners. He didn't speak a word until he was four years old. Thomas Edison, the classic delinquent youth, was once punished in the village square for building a fire in a barn. It is reputed that Dorothy Parker was expelled from parochial school for calling the Immaculate Conception the "Spontaneous Combustion." Wernher Von Braun, father of rocketry, flunked the equivalent of our ninth-grade algebra. In 1975, the National Science Foundation estimated that of the brightest 10 percent of American schoolchildren, over 125,000 drop out each year.[1]

It is true that every child has a gift: imagination, a quick wit, the ability to almost always hit that softball, a memory for faces, a sincere concern for other people, a love of music, a vast storehouse of specific facts and figures, a smile that melts your heart. Every child is of undeniable value to us all. Every child is a gifted child. But it is also true that some are more gifted than others. This second truth means that there is a group of children with mental and physical capabilities far beyond those normally seen in children of their equal years. The tragedy is that, by and large, these children are retarded or damaged by our educational and social systems. They struggle through curricula, lesson plans, workbooks and laboratory assignments all planned for someone else's needs and abilities. It's like spending your life in pants that don't fit.

In the classroom they are often misinterpreted. Underachievement is mistaken for low ability. Creative wit is dismissed as a lack of respect for others. Restlessness is equated with a need for discipline.

I remember Jason. Even at age five, he could sweep into a room and take over.

"What are you doing? What's this thing on your desk? How come you're doing that now? Do you have any gum? What day is this? You put that in the wrong place, it should be over here. Tie my shoe."

Most adults instantly disliked him. He asked too many questions; he demanded too many answers; he had no self-control. But he was intelligently gifted. And when given a project of sufficient challenge, he could spend an entire day in self-directed study.

It has taken society far too long to recognize that children with retarded mental and physical abilities require special education and focus if they are to develop to their total capacities. Thank God we've brought them out of the attics and cellars. This basic right has yet to be unanimously extended to children on the opposite end of the developmental scale.

Ruth Martinson, professor of psychology at California State College and an advocate of special education for the gifted, has observed: "We must be willing to say that people, even very young people, are unequal; that they are different in talents and abilities. The public schools are obligated to recognize these differences."[2]

Before we can discuss ways to help our GCs we have to dispel some lingering myths.

MYTH: All children are equal and should be treated alike.

TRUTH: All children are equal in value—but they are not all alike. They should not be treated as if they were.

MYTH: GCs are smart enough to learn everything by themselves.

TRUTH: Without an educational system that keeps pace with their abilities to absorb quickly and assimilate large amounts of data, and without emotional support and encouragement, GCs fail. With failure and the ensuing low self-image, they can turn their gifts to negative and destructive pursuits.

MYTH: The GC is a rare anomaly and can easily be spotted because he (1) recites logarithms, (2) has a photographic memory, (3) speaks in deep abstractions, (4) is weird or close to insanity, (5) all of the above.

TRUTH: There are hundreds of thousands of GCs who go unidentified and thus unhelped because of apathy, poor screening techniques and general misunderstandings regarding how intelligence develops.

MYTH: To recognize GCs is to set them apart. This is undemocratic and elitist.

TRUTH: I'm so sick of the hysteria over elitism! It is patently elitist and discriminatory to deny GCs their equal rights to an appropriate education and social support simply because they are what they are.

There are a few lucky ones. Gifted athletes and talented artists are encouraged in our society. We pay them to delight us. But gifted intellectuals and scholars aren't particularly entertaining—so we accuse them of trying to be superior. No one is threatened by a great fast-ball pitcher; but everyone fears being "outsmarted." Supporting gifted education is not giving sanction to genetic perversion. Nobody says we're going to mate these kids after the graduation dance. Let's finally bury that Super Race bugaboo and get on with rearing our kids to be the best they can be.

MYTH: You either have it or you don't.

TRUTH: We don't really know the truth of this statement. There are as many theories on the origin of genius as there are on the origin of taco stands. Some experts say it is totally inherited; some say it is learned and developed; some say it has to do with the mysteries of mothers' milk; while some say it is an intricate interweaving of related abilities and potentialities (and that just means they don't know either). We do believe that there are many kinds of giftedness. We do believe it can usually be identified. And a lot of us believe it can be altered for the better or worse by education, environment, enlightenment or all of these.

EXPERT TESTIMONY

To understand the child who is advancing more rapidly than her peers, one must first understand the basic theories of normal child development. I can't argue with that. But I am like many parents: such thoughts never occurred to me. My conceptualization of child rearing was rather simplistic. Kids just grow up, that's all. You love them, feed them, "hose them off" once in a while, bandage any major wounds, attend school pageants, and they grow up.

When it first occurred to me we might be the parents of a GC, it got a bit more complex. Before I knew it, I was off the deep end. I pitched my copy of *The Better Homes & Garden*

Baby Book and plunged into *Piaget's Theory of Intellectual Development: An Introduction* and Erikson's *Childhood and Society*. I almost drowned, but the highlights were interesting.

A Swiss biologist born in 1896, Piaget studied many things, among them, the growth and development of human beings. He was one of the first prominent scientists to recognize that children are quite different from adults in three essential ways: their methods of approaching reality, their views of the world, their uses of language.

It seems difficult to believe in our child-oriented society, but Piaget's ideas were quite revolutionary. Until that time, children were thought to be miniature adults, with all of the same needs, motivations and desires. (It's hard to imagine that the average mom and dad thought that, but at least the "experts" did.)

Many of our modern educational methods are based upon Piaget's theories and concepts of child development. He believed that intelligence was the ability to organize information, remember it, and then adapt it to new situations. He hypothesized that memory can (1) change with age, (2) be adversely affected by environment, and (3) improve as a result of related intellectual skills.[3]

He divided the development of a normal infant into six stages:

Stage 1   0–1 month   *The use of reflexes*

Stage 2   1–4 months   *Acquired adaptations*
- examination of stationary objects in environment
- coordination of grasping and vision
- exploration of objects with mouth

Stage 3   5–7 months   *Beginning of intentional adaptations*
- a desire for gratification
- greater emergence of individual personality
- development of the concept of a stable environment, favorite toy, etc.
- beginning to search for and recover vanished objects (linking to reality)

Stage 4   8-12 months *Acquisition of instrumental behavior*
- emergence of genuinely intentional activities
- active search for vanished objects
- developing a means to an end
- imitation of a model

Stage 5   12-18 months *Discovery of new means*
- more exploration, particularly allowing objects to fall and throwing objects
- emergence of trial and error to solve problems
- imitation of actions never before performed by him
- looks for lost objects where last seen

Stage 6   18-24 months *Internal representation of action in the external world*
- great cognitive growth
- ability to picture events and follow them mentally
- trial and error not always necessary to achieve desired results

According to Piaget, the later stages of childhood were:

2-7 years *Preoperational period*
- disequilibrium in conceptual thinking
- self-contradictions
- most easy for others to underestimate or overestimate child's real abilities

7-11 years *Concerted operations*
- acquisition of rudiments of time, space, number and logic
- concepts of volume and density usually remain too difficult

His theory (and thousands of educators now claim to have practical verification) was that a child must pass through all stages in sequential order for optimal learning to take place. If a child skipped or was retarded at any stage, subsequent stages would drastically suffer.[4]

An example seems appropriate here. Reading is an extremely complex skill requiring physical coordination, intellect and memory. A GC of three or four years can have the intellect and memory necessary to accomplish the task. But this same child might have had physical coordination retarded at an earlier stage. Specifically, if she cannot continuously move her eyes in a left to right motion across a narrow space (line of type), she must then return to an earlier developmental stage to "pick up" the missing skill before more complex skills can be fully acquired. (Of course, in some instances, compensation takes over and the skill is never acquired. The classic example is the child who learns to read by sight/memorization rather than phonics and is forever handicapped by unfamiliar words and poor spelling.)[5]

Much educational research and a great many Ph.D. dissertations have followed. Two examples:

T. R. Bower constructed a schedule of motor developments for the normal child. These include:

	(Approximately)
Holds head up, prone	1–10 weeks
Rolls over	19–36 weeks
Sits alone	24–35 weeks
Stands holding furniture	33–49 weeks
Stands alone	49–75 weeks
Walks alone	50–75 weeks[6]

Abraham Maslow theorized that all humans develop because of motivations to fulfill a hierarchy of needs. Primary needs must be met before an individual will choose to pursue higher needs. A tremendously condensed listing of that hierarchy is as follows:

Physiological needs (oxygen, food, water, warmth)
Safety needs (these can readily be seen in the infant or child who reacts in either a defensive—retreating to a position of security—or offensive—screaming, throwing ob-

jects—manner when sensing danger, loud noises, movement, etc.)

Belongingness and love needs (hugging, physical comfort, cuddling)

Esteem needs (recognition, attention, respect)

Need for self-actualization (making one's own decisions, self-fulfillment)

Need to know and to understand

Aesthetic needs[7]

What You Really Came For

This brings us to children of rapid development. Absolutely everyone seems to have a special definition for giftedness. Lewis Terman published the often praised, often maligned tome, *Genetic Studies of Genius: Mental and Physical Traits of a Thousand Gifted Children,* in 1926, and it has been a free-for-all ever since.

In 1971, Sidney P. Marland, U.S. Commissioner of Education, prepared a report for the Congress in which gifted and talented children were defined as those children possessing outstanding abilities and capable of high performance in one or more of the following areas: "(1) general intellectual ability, (2) specific academic aptitude, (3) creative or productive thinking, (4) leadership ability, (5) visual and performing arts aptitude, and (6) psychomotor ability."[8] By and large, this official definition from the U.S. Office of Education remains the mainstay in current administrative decisions about the educational programs offered GCs. This document prompted the Congress to create the Office of Gifted and Talented, currently within the Bureau of Education of the Handicapped.

Six years later, the Gifted Child Act excluded appropriations for psychomotor abilities, and it was consequently excluded from many practical definitions of giftedness. There is little cause for alarm, however, since public schools, the American Legion and the Mystic Knights of Wherever have always provided more than adequate resources for children (especially males) who were gifted in the area of psychomotor skills. (Although usually interpreted as athletic ability, a psychomotor skill could also be the ability to speedread or type at a lightning pace.) In other words, none of us should lose sleep over decline in support for youth athletics. They have been and remain the only truly comprehensive gifted educational programs available to most children.

And so we are left with five basic areas that are considered when experts decide who is a GC.

1. *General intelligence.* My grandmother used to call it "common horse sense." It simply means knowing a great deal about a great many things, or at least being able to make an accurate guess. Very often the GC of general intelligence is a poor-to-average student. He may spend high school in the principal's office, drop out of college and end up owning a multinational chain of disco laundromats.

2. *Academic superiority.* Such superiority usually shows up in one or two specific subject areas. These are the children who "look" as if they should be GCs. They usually make good grades in school and are most often identified in teacher-based selection methods. All stereotypic jokes aside, these are the people responsible for most scientific advancements, industrial technology and medical miracles. God love them one and all, or the rest of us could still be struggling through life with wooden wheels and lukewarm Coca-Cola.

3. *Creativity.* This is, by far, the most difficult of any category to evaluate. It's the old chicken and egg story: does creative discovery lead to intelligence and aptitude, or must a person possess high levels of these skills in order to generate a creative thought? Don't you have to be creative to even recognize creativity? What is truly creative and what is modification of the known? Is there a difference?

The professional literature of educational testing generally shows a correlation of about 0.3 between high creativity scores and high IQ scores. (That's less than chance.) And yet, leaders in the field of gifted education stress the interdependence of these two skills in actual life situations.

Harold Hughes, in a journal article, "The Enhancement of Creativity," identifies creativeness as behavior that is dependent upon the following:

1. Selective memory
2. Divergent thinking
3. Introversion
4. Attraction to resolvable disorder (you know, those kids who love to untie knots in a wad of string)
5. Free time
6. Supportive climate
7. Self-discipline[9]

Gil Caudill, currently a consultant for the Blue River Special Education Co-op (Shelbyville, Indiana) and a pioneer consultant in the field of gifted education, relates creativity to nonconformity. Creative children, he believes, have no inclination to conform. But unlike their adult counterparts (the ones who survive), they are continually pressured and intimidated into the traditional molds.

Think back to your own school days. How many times was the class comic—perhaps a true creative genius—told to shut up and/or sit down? What kinds of social and authoritative pressures were brought to bear upon the kid who always came up with the craziest schemes to raise prom money? Who was kicked off the newspaper/yearbook staff for going "a bit too far"?

Every day, creativeness runs the educational gauntlet:

"Don't color out of the lines."
"Jimmy, dear, the sky is supposed to be blue and the grass green."
"Sweetheart, nobody ever heard of a skeleton with licorice bones."
"Sarah, we don't make our capital D's that way."
"No, no—the big blocks go here, and the little blocks go there."

4. *Leadership.* Abraham Lincoln entered the Black Hawk Wars an Army captain and emerged with the rank of private—obviously a man unfit for leadership. But leaders are undeniably gifted—even if we have a difficult time defining the parameters of their special talents.

It really isn't a fluke that one student in a class of 1500 high school freshmen is elected class president. According to James Gallagher, an educational administrator specializing in giftedness, "It is possible to say on the basis of available research that gifted children are, as a group, almost invariably more popular and more socially accepted than children of other levels of intellectual ability."[10]

GCs run the street gangs, dominate nursery schools and are the undisputed rulers of the neighborhood playground. They decide who selects the kick-ball team. They decide what will be "the" latest school wardrobe necessity. And every teacher worth his salt knows that it's "rule or be ruled" when it comes to the social leader of any classroom.

5. *Visual/performing arts.* While acclaim in the arts is subjective and dependent upon many social factors, talent and ability are perceived as being apparent to many of us. "I don't know much about art, but. . ." Those children with early and profound talents are particularly easy to identify. When we hear a six-year-old piano prodigy, we know we have heard a GC. The child star of a Broadway musical is easy to spot. And while art teachers maintain that composition and mathematical precision can be taught, an elementary student who can accurately sketch a horse, or a landscape, or a human form is a GC who needs special education if those talents are to be refined.

It is here that one of the most glaring flaws in current methods of identification of GCs becomes apparent. It didn't take me long to recognize the great amount of energy expended by the "experts" as they try to devise a single system that will absolutely, positively, always and for all times identify every child with any degree of giftedness. No such system yet exists. Identifying children with special educational needs remains a time-consuming, individualistic approach. You can't single them out as easily as you can spot ripe tomatoes. Meanwhile children who are, as Caudill calls them, "terminally gifted," go unattended. Joyce Van Tassell, 1980 president of the Association for the Gifted, cautions educators about ignoring the "severely and profoundly gifted" while squabbling over semantics and the vague distinctions between "gifted ability" and "superior-average ability."

So What's New?

Joseph Renzulli, a nationally recognized leader in the field, defines giftedness as the interdependence of three "clusters" of behavior traits. His concept is illustrated in a three-ring model.[11] Above average ability, task commitment and creativity are equal ingredients in the accomplishment we label gifted and talented.

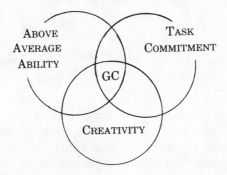

Emerging definitions now stress the need to identify potentiality rather than rely on statistical norms and single-standard test scores to measure achievement. Under these definitions far greater numbers of children are being identified as being gifted and talented.

Many of the old beliefs about totally inherited patterns of mental growth have been shattered by the successes in expanding environmental and educational advantages.[12] We may not be able to create a gift, but we certainly have the educational resources to broaden and refine it. Belief in this concept is essential if you, as a parent, have any intention of becoming involved in the growth and development of your GC. If you don't believe in this concept, skip all the trauma over your child's education and concentrate upon finding an appropriate GC-in-law.

Handstands at Six Months
and Other Developmental Differences

By and large, GCs seem to be a healthy lot. The earliest and probably the most comprehensive examination of physical characteristics of GCs was the 1926 Terman study.[13] In the chapter "Anthropometric Measurements" by Bird T. Baldwin the following conclusions were drawn:

> The GCs studied were above normal in physical growth stages for average height and weight.
> The group as a whole was physically superior to other study groups.*

Chapter 8 of Terman's study dealt with "Health and Physical History" and included the following observations about the studied GCs:

1. Only 4.4 percent were born prematurely.
2. The mean birth weight was ¾ pound above normal.
3. Walking averaged 1 month earlier and talking averaged 3.5 months earlier than the mean ages for normal children.
4. The GCs seemed to engage in more hours of daily sleep than did the control group.
5. GCs entered puberty at an earlier age than did other children.

No significant differences were found between the GCs and the normal control group in the following areas: frequency of colds, and frequency of contagious diseases.

Terman also made note of what appeared to be higher levels of daily nutrition, a longer period of breast feeding and

---

* For years this concept virtually excluded any GC with physical handicaps, learning disabilities, or birth defects. I include it here because of its historic impact on educational thought—*not* because of its truth. Your GC may have any of a number of disabilities.

The special needs of handicapped GCs require much greater depth than is possible in this chapter.

significantly lower instances of defective hearing among the GCs. Subsequent research has certainly verified and expanded upon the consequences of these factors in human development. Children with hearing deficiencies have, until recently, been erroneously excluded from groups of GCs simply because testing instruments were unable to measure accurately their real abilities. Finally, the Terman study reported about a quarter more cases of vision problems in the group of GCs.

Much controversy exists over Terman's conclusions. Although 1000 is a respectable research subject number, the study was limited to GCs with similar ethnic backgrounds, economic environments and geographic experiences. It was also limited to GCs whose parents were interested enough to drag them back to the clinic for repeated and extensive observation. *But*—to date, no other scientific study of genius with such depth exists. The impact of the study was something akin to the birth of a messiah. Even Terman's own follow-up study (1945) could not completely dispel educational theories and methodologies spawned by his earlier conclusions.

Two significantly smaller but detailed studies of GCs have also produced some interesting generalizations. Please accept them as generalizations—not gospel.

Leta Hollingworth studied in great depth ten children who had been tested at above 180 on the Stanford-Binet Intelligence Test. Some conclusions were:

- Median age of walking—14 months.
- Median age of talking—14 months.
- Median age of reading—3 years.[14]

In a 1979 study of ten children enrolled in a gifted preschool program, Frankie H. Cooper obtained the following averages from parental interviews:

- Birth weight—6.85 pounds.
- Age walked—11.8 months.
- Age crawled—7.86 months.
- Age talked—9.45 months.
- Age first read—4.64 years.[15]

Studies by many researchers seem to indicate that physical differences between gifted and average children are not as startling as were earlier thought to be true. In "Physiques of Gifted Children and Their Less Gifted Siblings," Laycock and Caylor challenge the conclusions of the Terman study as being naïve in light of new knowledge in the fields of nutrition and environmental toxicity.[16]

Obviously, any discussion of the physical advancement of GCs cannot exclude the factors of environmental health. Are certain children physically and/or mentally superior as an incident of birth, or are they products of environment, nutrition and even economic privilege? The professionals call it the nature-nurture controversy. To an outside observer it resembles the way they must have chosen up sides in a Holy War. "Okay, all you believers over here with the Normans; all you infidels over there with the Saxons." As with religion, you either believe it or you don't. Gifts and talents are primarily inherited or they are primarily factors of environment. While reading the literature on the controversy, I was taken by what seemed to be a hesitancy to even mention the word heredity in the same sentence with giftedness. Perhaps it is a reaction to past abominations in the name of genetics. Perhaps it is a professional self-service to stress the power of the classroom. I frankly don't know. But for me, the argument is of little consequence. I tend to be a bet-hedger. Since I can't alter my GC's genes the way I do his pants, I plan to teach him what I consider good nutritional habits, purge our household of as many "edible" chemicals as I can, have him floss his teeth, never buy his shoes too tight and keep him out of drafts. It can't hurt!

Emotional Stability

Then there's that little matter of genius being next to insanity. We've had enough sexist remarks about old wives—but this tale is truly ridiculous.

At the beginning of this chapter you were introduced to Charles. He was real. And there are most certainly others like him: the genius gone mad—intellect out of control—a cunning manipulation of people and events. It is a chilling thought. But the fear of GCs like Charles is far greater than their actual number.

Although every population subgroup contains a percentage of individuals who behave in ways unacceptable to general society (be they violent deviates or amusing eccentrics), educational research is full of examples of how GCs are usually as emotionally stable as are other children. In fact, James Gallagher, an administrator with the Superintendent of Public Instruction, Illinois, has stated, "The evidence available regarding the superior emotional adjustment of the intellectually gifted child seems very strong. It is found consistently whether the measuring instruments are teachers' ratings or personality tests."[17]

Even Terman, in follow-up to his classic studies, tried to dispel the myth: "Results of thirty years' follow-up of these subjects by field studies in 1927–1928, 1939–1940 and 1951–1952, and by mail follow-up at other dates show that the incidence of mortality, ill health, insanity and alcoholism is in each case below that for the generality of corresponding age . . . and that the delinquency rate is but a fraction of what it is in the general public."[18]

I have described GCs as being extremely sensitive to environmental stimuli. When these stimuli are negative and hostile, the results follow in a logical manner. Charles was a genius. He was also a battered child, sexually abused by his biological mother. He did not know his real father and he was shuttled from one foster home to another.

There are questions that none of us can avoid. What happens when any child is poisoned rather than nurtured? If a GC comes from an environment that is devoid of support, encouragement or respect, who else can help? The legal system? The school? The community? When there is no communal recognition, acceptance or attendance of GCs in general, it is the specific GC like Charles who slips through the cracks and surfaces again in ways to give us all a common nightmare.

The crucial point is that madness is not the step after genius on the intellectual continuum. Madness is far more complicated than that. Nevertheless, the gifted do have special emotional needs that are thought to be directly related to their unique abilities.

GCs are very often terrified of failure. This behavior can be manifested in several negative ways:

> The overwhelming (and terribly annoying) need to be always right.
> An avoidance of competitive situations *when victory cannot be assured.*
> A reluctance to be adventurous or to try new experiences.

I remember Jeff. At age nine, Jeff was both intellectually and athletically gifted. He was at the top of his class in school. His reading, math and analytical skills were so advanced that everyone knew that Jeff always got every answer correct. At recess, he won all the footraces, climbed the highest and always hit the ball. At this point you're saying, "So what's the problem?" The problem was that Jeff was unhappy. His parents were baffled at his increasing depression and resistance to attending school. They made a special trip to the school and there they learned the answer. Jeff's teacher had observed that he was particularly despondent during and after art class. A casual check of Jeff's locker revealed a cache of old art assignments and projects. He had never taken any of his art work home to show his parents. Later he told them that his drawings and crafts just weren't good enough for them to see. He demanded perfection of himself and art class was his first faint indication that he might not be perfect. Parents of GCs must be ever on guard for the subtle but destructive signs of the fear of failure.

When they are not identified and given needed support, GCs often develop below average self-images. The differences they perceive between themselves and other children can be interpreted in negative ways. GCs who make it to adulthood often describe childhoods filled with fears and self-doubts. "I thought something was wrong with me. I never seemed to like what the other kids liked; I always felt 'out of it.' "

Young GCs can discern the details of interpersonal relationships long before they are able to explain historically or rationalize gross inconsistencies. Concepts such as politeness, etiquette, social pecking orders, injustice, prejudice, etc., are extremely frustrating because they are so illogical.

GCs are often emotionally disturbed by the unanswerable questions of the cosmos and must continually be assured of their individual places in time and space. They must maintain a constant point of reference. "Who am I now?" "Where are we now?" "How is this like what happened before?" are common questions.

These characteristics can become quite serious if left unattended. They present one of the most tragic ways in which the needs of the GC can go unmet. Such needs aren't always obvious. Unlike physically handicapped or mentally retarded children, GCs often don't "look like" they need help until it is far too late.

BEHAVIORAL CLUES

It is part of the joy of being a parent to be overwhelmed and elated with each child's every accomplishment. The entire "baby's first journal" industry is based upon the fact that we love to record baby's first sound, baby's first smile, baby's first step and baby's first blood blister.

In an exhaustive study spanning seventeen years, Harvard professor Burton White researched the issue of how to build upon these early experiences and accomplishments. He stressed the fact that "in their simple everyday activities, infants and toddlers form the foundations of all later development."[19]

The early identification of giftedness is particularly necessary if parents are to take advantage of those crucial first years of growth and development. Standardized testing and expert verification of a child's giftedness can be inconclusive below the ages of 2½ to 3 years. But giftedness starts at day one. Parents and family members can daily observe the rapid developments and behavioral clues of a budding GC.

Yet, the GC often eludes recognition. First there's that little matter of social pressure to suppress accomplishment. It often goes like this: You're talking to your sister-in-law and she naturally asks about the baby (now eleven months old).

"Well, she did the cutest thing today—we were watching 'Sesame Street' and I'm sure she pointed to the TV and said 'duck.' "

Your sister-in-law laughs, sloughs it off, attributing the story to new motherness, and proceeds to tell you her secret of the perfect meat loaf.

Often parents are unsure as to the specific ways in which their child deviates from the norm. It's very easy to dismiss the signs. After all, every book you read and every pediatrician in the world say that all children are different. Few sources will go so far as to tell you how different. If you have had little exposure to other children (or if you simply don't pay attention), it's easy to assume that all children behave like GCs. They do not.

Some experts say that the GC goes through all normal developmental stages—just a little sooner or with more intensity. The tantrums of the "terrible twos" can come at eleven months. Reading can be accomplished at age three rather than the usual five or six years. It seems to be a difference in rate of development rather than in type of development.[20]

Dorothy Sisk, former Director of the Office of Gifted and Talented (OGT), U.S. Office of Education, has published a list of guideposts for those parents who suspect they have a GC.

1. Early use of advanced vocabulary.
2. Keen observation and curiosity.
3. Retention of a variety of information.
4. Periods of intense concentration.
5. Ability to understand complex concepts, perceive relationships and think abstractly.
6. A broad and changing spectrum of interests.
7. Strong critical thinking skills and self-criticism.
8. Early demonstration of talents in music, art, athletics and/or the performing arts.[21]

Now, I know that a great deal of consideration went into that list. The OGT had only one thought in mind: to help parents. At the early stages of recognition, parents of GCs need re-inforcement. More than anything else, they want to be assured that their observations are indeed valid. But frankly, I had a hard time relating to such generalized concepts.

Whenever I meet the parents of a GC, I always slip in the question: "How did you first know?" I've used their answers and my own observations to translate that list into descriptions of daily activities.

Don't forget: few children exhibit all characteristics of gift-edness at all times. And please, no letters about how I can't talk specifics because every child is an individual. Of course every child is an individual; we all know that by now. But without some specific and definitive examples, how can you reach any comparative conclusions?

READING THE PAMPERS BOX
(*Early Use of Advanced Vocabulary*)

There is no question that many GCs first exhibit giftedness by an early command of the language. And this includes self-taught reading.

Speech begins in the infant as a series of reflex motor char-acteristics (crying, sucking and swallowing). It then progresses through the stages of:

1. Reflex sounds
2. Babbling (goo-goo, gah-gah)
3. Socialized vocal play (mimicking vowels and double syl-lables, da-da)
4. First words (imitation of others is the key here)
5. Phrases and sentences
6. Refinement of articulation, voice, rhythm and language

As our son began early speech (a distinct "no" at seven months), I scoured the bookcases for some detailed information on "normal" speech development. An old text from a college course in speech pathology revealed: "At eighteen months, the child's speech activity consists of a few meaningful words. . . .

Some typical examples, are: ... bye-bye ... mama ... and dink (for drink)."[22]

If your eighteen-month-old has a vocabulary including dog, ball, cold, shoe, Coke, radio and/or transistor, you should suspect something. (The "r" sound is particularly difficult to master, as exemplified by the number of first-graders who anxiously await the Easter "wabbit.") A three-year-old whose vocabulary includes such words as "marvelous," "invisible," "conscious," "determine" and "professional" is probably a GC. A three-year-old who uses these words properly in spontaneous conversation most certainly is.

(A sidebar to activists in the nature-nurture controversy: Friends and relatives used to tease me over a ritual I developed with our infant GC. After each feeding I would spend some of our cuddling time slowly and clearly reciting the phonetic alphabet. As his verbal abilities began to surface, some of them were taking it a bit more seriously.)

As with many topics regarding child-rearing, "teaching a child to read" generates much debate. Some educators admonish the parent not to sanction, push or bribe a child into early reading. Worst of all is the implanted fear that we can somehow teach our children in the "wrong way"—thus causing confusion, negativism and severe bed-wetting when the child must relearn the correct (teacher's) way. Others call this reasoning primitive and turn to such books as "Teaching Your Infant to Read" and "A Toddler's Introduction to Shakespeare." I suspect there is no single correct answer. As is true about many skills, we know that reading has been successfully taught when the child successfully reads. Everyone from the YMCA to Esther Williams has an idea of the proper way to teach a child to swim. All that really matters is not drowning.

Nevertheless, it was a moot point for us. Our GC taught himself to read the Pampers box. It started as he began identifying logos in newspaper ads. We thought it charming he could spot the Dunkin' Donut Girl and recite slogans (obviously heard on TV). One day, he pointed to the words "the boy" and told me that he was a boy too. My initial reaction was shock. I even accused his father of ventriloquism. Ever the skeptic, I gathered his favorite picture books and began a little informal testing session. "What's this word?" "What does that say?" And he was correct.

I suspect it came about because of our nightly ritual of bedtime stories. Since he and I are both insomniacs, it often went on for hours. After becoming incredibly bored with his favorites (I was particularly hostile toward talking animals), I selfishly moved on to heavier, yet entertaining fare: Eudora Welty, Faulkner, *National Geographic* (he did like the pictures) and, when I was in the mood, an occasional Tolstoy.

I don't pretend to know how it happened; but obviously, any child first learns those things to which he is most exposed. His favorite was a Richard Scarry book in which cute little everyday objects are neatly labeled. This explains nouns and verbs—simple association and a good memory. I have no explanation for articles, contractions, pronouns and prepositions.

"Why?" "How Do You Know?"
(Keen Observation and Curiosity)

Our son always asks questions in tandem. "Why?" followed by a terse but brilliant parental response, and "How do you know?" followed by, "Because I said so."

All children go through stages of intense curiosity, but GCs have an insatiable mental appetite for *every* minute detail of *everything*.

They open drawers and cupboards when you visit relatives. They question sales clerks; follow the meter reader through the yard; ask the grocery clerk how the cash register operates; look under the counters at K-Mart; tear apart Christmas toys to "see how they work"; demand an explanation of all the dental equipment while you're having your teeth cleaned; and ask you to explain in detail, this minute, every concept that is unfamiliar.

One memorable conversation I had with our four-year-old GC comes to mind.

HE: What holds up a building?
ME: I don't know, the foundation and wood and steel things in the walls.

HE: You mean steal, like taking something?

ME: No, S-T-E-E-L. That kind of steel is a hard metal and they use it to make buildings.

HE: What's a foundation?

ME: The foundation is the very bottom part of the building. It's made out of something hard like concrete or bricks, and the building rests on it.

HE: Rests? How can a building sleep?

ME: No, sleep is only one kind of rest. Rest can also mean to sit upon. Like a building sits upon a foundation.

HE: How is the wood used?

ME: The walls and roof of a building are first outlined in wooden boards or steel beams; all the pieces push against each other, and the rest of the building is added on.

HE: Like a skeleton?

ME: Right! [A breakthrough!] Yes, a building has a skeleton-like structure just as people have bones.

HE: Wood comes from trees, right?"

ME: Right.

HE: What holds up a tree?

ME: Ask your father.

"AND THEN FONZIE SAID ..."
(Retention of a Variety of Information)

It goes beyond remembering. In college, I knew a guy who could tell a movie. He would stand in the student union and literally tell an entire movie—from the opening scene to the credits. He would recite all the roles (many in character); give stage directions; describe viewpoint and motivation; detail wardrobes and sketch in scenic design. I once watched almost two hours while he told *The Graduate* to a crowd. It wasn't until years later when I saw the film that I realized the extent of his talent.

Many GCs can recite the libretto of *Peter and the Wolf* or recall the details of last year's birthday party. Seth's mother tells me she is constantly apologizing to the teachers because her GC recites episodes of "Gulligan's Island" for show and tell.

"He really doesn't watch TV all the time," she will plead. They never believe her. And when she and Seth go to the grocery, he sings the commercial for every product she puts into the basket.

GCs of four or five years often combine this skill with the common (though somewhat later) fascination many children have with monsters. Instead of dwelling upon vague, mythical monsters like Puff or Godzilla, young GCs memorize the names of dinosaurs. One of our son's most frustrating periods was the time it took me to learn the difference between a Pterodactyl and a Pteranodon. (I mean, for goodness' sake, they both flew, didn't they?)

The mother of one GC tells me her daughter can remember (in detail, of course) every outfit she wore on every school day of an entire year. And I know of another GC who always helps her mother shop for groceries. She comes in handy because she can remember all the prices from the previous trip.

More often than not, this fabulous memory is only called upon for subjects of interest. So, the fifth-grader who can't remember when Columbus sailed the ocean blue can remember the rushing statistics of the Pittsburgh backfield.

PLEASE GOD—NO MORE STAR WARS
(Periods of Intense Concentration)

I've had it with intergalactic travel and extraterrestrial beings. I'm giving fair warning to Luke, Han, Buck, Spock and Commander Adama—don't ever cross my laserpath. Our GC is, as they say, "into science fiction." He has, if fact, spent the better part of the past three years reading sci-fi, building space vehicles, studying astronomy, peering through his telescope, composing cosmic music, looking for bits of meteors in the gravel along roadsides and planning his Halloween costumes. I sometimes feel I have to put on my green head, just to get his attention.

Such intense concentration can be manifest in many ways. I heard of a GC who spent months studying grasshoppers. He knew all the species, their habitats, life cycles and role in folklore. He culminated his research by constructing a 3-foot grass-hopper model to anatomical perfection.

Your GC probably collects something, anything: rocks, Happy Meal boxes, shells, model planes, dolls or pictures of Willie Nelson.

This concentration is also seen in periods of study and isolation. A GC will often spend several hours of each day sequestered in his room. GCs are more receptive to stimuli than are normal children. They receive and perceive almost everything. Many experts in the field of gifted education believe that this time of seclusion and meditation is essential for the GC to assimilate and categorize all the images that bombard him. Many classrooms for the GC will feature a tent or cave in which they can elect to simply sit and be alone.

"WOULD YOUR SECOND COUSIN'S DAUGHTER
BE MY THIRD COUSIN ONCE REMOVED?"
(*The Ability to Understand Complex Concepts,
Perceive Relationships and Think Abstractly*)

Every IQ test seems to utilize the intrafamily relationship as a problem in complex logic. It's based upon familiar concepts and it's very complicated. (Ever try to introduce relatives to your spouse at a family reunion?) GCs delight in such problems.

They also love to untie the knots in a wad of string, work crossword puzzles, connect-the-dots and play with video games. They often display an early and intense fascination with time and money. "What day is it?" "How many minutes until we eat?" "How many days have I been alive?" "How many nickels are in $1.85?" "How many hours did it take to make the sofa?" All of these illustrate the ability to understand complex concepts and perceive relationships.

Sometimes they're just too smart. Shannon's parents bought her a wristwatch as a motivational carrot for teaching her to tell time. Periodically they would ask: "Shannon, what time is it now?" Watch-on-wrist, she would walk into their bedroom for a glance at the digital clock.

In addition, your GC will be fascinated with other abstract

concepts such as love, hate, truth and the cycles of life. He will ask who made the world (usually while you're on line at the deli or trying to buy underwear). She will be particularly skillful at drawing analogies. He will notice the inconsistencies of life: "Why is that woman eating? She's too fat already." And one little manifestation of this skill we all hate to recognize is the GC's exceptional skills at lying and the fine art of manipulation.

Finally, an intense capacity for abstract thought can become detrimental. Tasks (particularly tasks attempted before physical maturation) can become too intellectualized, and thus never accomplished.

There was that disastrous summer we wanted our three-year-old GC to swim. I know there are thousands of infants and toddlers floating and swimming this very moment. At three, our son was not physically ready. He watched the instructor; he watched the swimmers; he tried with all he was worth, and he sank every time. His frustration and sense of personal failure were heartbreaking.

The afternoon he sat at poolside and cried, "I know *how* to swim, my body just won't do it" did it for me. We spent the rest of the season on terra firma.

"THAT WAS LAST WEEK."
(*A Broad and Changing Spectrum of Interests*)

There is that "variety/spice of life" equation, but sometimes the GC can flutter from subject to subject with little direction or substantive learning. This is most apparent in the GC who spends an entire weekend at a jigsaw puzzle, the next week researching South American Indian cultures, the following week listening to only Irish folk music. Or, she will become totally engulfed in a hobby for a relatively long period only to emerge reciting the word "nevermore." (This most often occurs *after* you've bought next year's Christmas presents.)

It is a basic challenge of gifted education to teach the GC to attend to and complete specific tasks. It may be called boredom, immaturity, sensitivity to sensory distraction or downright contrariness. The result is the same—many GCs simply never learn to finish a task. They easily absorb what they want from a situation and move on. On a philosophical level, there may be nothing immoral or destructive about this. On a practical level, a child who will be living with other human beings in any type of society will have a hard life with such habits.

OUTGUESSING MR. ROGERS
(Strong Critical Skills and Self-Criticism)

Some GCs are their own most fervent critics. They can be perfectionists who possess such strong self-motivational drives that nothing they do seems to please them. As a parent, these can be difficult times. When do you tell a child to acccept less? How do you convince her that what she has accomplished is adequate even though not perfect?

Meanwhile, the quality of tenacity or persistence has long been identified as an essential element to learning.[23] The child who can't "stick with it" will only learn to move on to an easier project.

Achieving a balance between working to your utmost capacity and backing off before you self-destruct is difficult for many adults. And we've supposedly had a lot more practice.

The quality of critical thinking—so essential to creative and higher thought processes—can result in some different behavior patterns for a young GC.

Sometimes their insistence upon accuracy of detail can be maddening. Most notably, your GC will not allow you to make the socially acceptable, but gross, contradictions in everyday logic. Don't ask him to eat "a couple" of carrots, when you mean three or four (that's "several"). Don't ask her to "wait a minute" when you mean half an hour. The director of our son's school relayed a case in point. She was telling the five-year-olds a St. Patrick's Day story of the leprechauns.

"A leprechaun is a tiny little man, about six or seven inches high," she said. "And if you catch him, you get to keep his pot of gold."

One GC was not impressed.

"I don't see what's the big deal. If he's six inches tall, his pot of gold could only be about the size of a walnut."

(The kid was quick, but he didn't know the gold market.)

Our GC is still bitter over the Easter incident. When he was three, he overheard my plans to buy his "Easter outfit." He was unusually cooperative as he bathed and dressed to go shopping. After trying on two or three suits, he burst into a tantrum. He had envisioned an "Easter outfit" as a pink rabbit suit with ears "this long."

In addition, GCs can be extremely critical of others. This will be manifest by passive avoidance of the "offenders" or blatant intolerance, depending upon each child's personality.

One year I found myself involved in a neighborhood babysitting co-op. Stuart was four at the time and very gregarious with the children in his gifted preschool. The co-op seemed like a great way for him to meet new friends. My first assignment was to keep two brothers (ages four and six) while their mother went shopping. The boys spent 2½ hours in what seemed to me to be joyous harmony. That afternoon, as the brothers raced to their car, the mother made some of the obligatory social remarks:

"Thanks so much for keeping the boys. Stuart, you'll have to come to our house to play one afternoon."

With absolute sincerity my GC answered, "No, I don't think so. Your sons are too stupid. They don't seem to know much of anything."

My knees still weaken when I recall the wave of humiliation that hit me at that moment. Ever want to strangle your own kid?

I believe that three essential lessons for all GCs are (1) they exist in an imperfect world; (2) they themselves are imperfect; (3) parents made mistakes too.

(But more of that in the chapter entitled "Education, Like Charity, Begins at Home.")

She Only Sings Harmony
(*Early Demonstration of Talents*)

You can see it whenever you observe any group of young children. One always runs faster, climbs higher, sings louder, plays to the crowd or attacks fingerpainting with more intensity.

When he was four, Jack's parents were told he was retarded in the development of his fine motor skills. So, they came upon the idea of piano lessons. Learning to read music would surely be a challenge since he could already read anything in English that interested him. What could be more perfect for strengthening those tiny finger muscles? Neater than Play-Doh, more appropriate than learning to be a masseur—the piano seemed perfect.

After several months, he reached what was to be a benchmark in his musical maturation. Jack learned to play "Yankee Doodle." "Jingle Bells," "Willy the Whale," "Happy Birthday"—these were passing amusements. But something serious clicked with "Yankee Doodle." For almost 1½ years he played "Yankee Doodle," every day: "Yankee Doodle" at middle C, upper C and lower C. He played "Yankee Doodle" on school pianos, pianos of the plastic toy variety, pianos that sat in the homes of their friends. He crawled into the display window at Baldwin's and played "Yankee Doodle" on a baby grand. He played "Yankee Doodle" in B-flat, and "Yankee Doodle" in double-time, pedals up, pedals down. He played "Yankee Doodle" backward. His favorite was to simultaneously play with left and right hands an octave apart.

"This whole thing may have been a mistake," his mother once told me. "In twenty years, he'll end up playing 'Yankee Doodle' to a bunch of drunks in a piano bar."

She could have just as well tried to change the rotation of the earth. This passion for and understanding of music were as innate to Jack as were the shapes of his fingernails. GCs bestowed with superior potentialities in art, music, self-expression and athletics usually cannot hold back the tide. They tap out rhythms with their pencils when they're supposed to be taking a history exam. They doodle in the margins of their philosophy notes. One successful novelist was quoted as saying, "If I were locked in a closet, I'd write on the walls."

If your GC expresses such a talent, nurture it, but don't waste your time trying to decide what to do with it. It's something out of your control.

And let us not forget wit and humor. At five our GC suddenly turned into Henny Youngman. I reached a point where I could "knock-knock" no longer. I remember those old jokes with motherly nostalgia though, particularly the one tag line that was paraphrased because of a bit of refreshing naïveté about animal husbandry:

"What do you get when you cross the road with a dog and a giraffe?" (A watch dog for the second floor.)

Those awful jokes really do mean something. Educators often refer to "Bloom's Taxonomy." With the assistance of college and university examiners, Benjamin Bloom compiled a list of optimum educational standards. The taxonomy suggests five universal goals for all educational programs:

1. Evaluation
2. Synthesis
3. Analysis
4. Application
5. Knowledge[24]

Every lesson plan, every lecture, every homework assignment should lead a child through these five objectives.

Creating the lowly pun is a classic culmination of the first three goals. Then, in order to bloom, the child needs only to (1) tax someone else (not "tax-on-a-me") and (2) retain the experience. (Who could forget?)

And GCs often demonstrate humor because their thought processes are so purely logical. Without digressing into the nature of humor, let's start with the premise that things are often funny when they're unexpected (a pratfall, a punch line, a pie in the face). Since we are surrounded by a largely illogical behavioral environment, the clear observations of a GC can stand out.

I remember Kurt. A TV reporter had been asked to discuss her vocation with a group of five- and six-year-old GCs. After a bit of the who, what, when, where story, she said, "The main thing a reporter must do is always tell the truth. I must report exactly and only what I see. My boss, the editor, tells me to come back to the studio with the facts—no lies or falsehoods—

just the truth. For example, what if I went on an assignment and tried to make up facts just to provide a more interesting story? What if I were doing a story about a farm and I told my editor that I had seen cows, chickens and a horse? And what if I tried to make up some more interesting facts and said that the horse had only three legs? What would my editor say to me?"

Kurt looked up with new interest. Completely deadpan he theorized, "He'd say that horse couldn't stand up."

When You Think You've Got One

When parents believe they have observed several of these behavioral characteristics, Dorothy Sisk recommends that they do the following:

Meet with your child's teacher. "Don't be discouraged if the teacher is unable to help; some school systems have not yet recognized the need to provide special services for the gifted." (*Amen,* Dorothy.)

Meet with the school counselors or administrator responsible for testing and bring a list of your observations and anecdotes. (Good luck on that one!)

Investigate community resources.[25] (Some good information here; often, the education or psychology department of a local college and/or university can put you in touch with the people in your community who are pioneering gifted education. *And* parents are beginning to organize and provide their own enrichment programs for GCs. Much more to follow on both topics.)

What If I'm Wrong?

At the time, taking our child to a psychologist for intelligence testing reminded me of those parents who drag their kids off to modeling agencies and casting calls. Any kid can eat cereal and flash a toothless grin. Any kid looks cute in Winnie-the-Pooh clothes. My kid can sing the Oscar Mayer Bologna song. I just don't want him contaminated by the shallow glitter and easy money of tinseltown. I admit to my prejudices. And some of those same stereotypes and biases were mingled in my thoughts of preschool testing.

I would have endless (and possibly neurotic) debates with myself:

"What makes you think your kid is so smart?"

"He's three years old and he reads the newspaper."

"Is that all?"

"He doesn't sound like other kids, he's different—more verbal—more inquisitive—more logical—his nose doesn't run all the time."

"You're his mother."

"But I'm also an intelligent, responsible adult. I can see that he's different."

"What are you going to do if they say he's a genius?"

"Nobody talks like that anymore."

"What are you going to do if they say he's highly gifted?"

"I'll have to find a special school—or join a group or something."

"What if he flunks the tests?"

"It doesn't matter. I just have to know for certain."

The discovery of a GC can happen in one of three ways:

1. The child is routinely evaluated in the school setting.
2. Parents suspecting giftedness arrange for private screening by a clinical psychologist or an educator with a doctorate in child psychology, tests and measurements, educational psychology or counseling.
3. Parents suspecting giftedness simply decide their kid "is one" and proceed from there.

It's the uncertainty that can be maddening. You know your child will be no different the hour after professional evaluation; you just want someone to give you an unbiased confirmation of what you've been thinking.

Don't be ashamed of what may seem to be mere personal

gratification. If the question has entered your mind, there are many sound, logical reasons why you must seek resolution:

1. Early diagnosis can help you make the most appropriate decisions for your child's special learning needs.
2. With "officialization" your child can be considered for any of the pioneering preschool developmental programs for the gifted.
3. With "officialization" you can remove your personal hesitancies or rationalizations and get on with reality.
4. It is undeniably true that giftedness can atrophy and/or regress without proper stimulation and direction. If this concerns you, there's no sense in wasting time.
5. It is also true that a first-grader reading on a fourth-grade level can have a negative adjustment to school unless parents and teachers are alert and responsive.
6. For the same reason you counted her toes—you have a right to know. Who says you're going to change her name to "Gigi" for Girl Genius or needlepoint an IQ plaque for his room?

And if you have a healthy, bright but not technically "gifted" child, so what? You have gained new and valuable information about someone to whom you are totally dedicated. Your awareness and sensitivity to his special nature and unique needs will never go wasted or unused.

Where do you go to have a young child tested for possible genius? They don't have such facilities in most shopping malls. Some possibilities:

1. Call the administrative office of your local school system. Ask if they have a program for gifted and talented children, get the name of the director or consultant, then ask for a referral to a professional evaluator.
2. Call the department of education of the nearest university or college and ask for advice.
3. If you live near a large city, consult the telephone directory under educational consultants, psychologists (be careful here—some of these may only want to focus on

why you're so concerned), schools and anything else you can think of. Call and ask questions.

4. Contact the
   U.S. Office of Education, Office of Gifted and Talented
   Donohue Building
   400 Sixth St. S.W., Room 3835
   Washington, DC 20202
   Toll-free Hotline: 1-800-424-2861

Some other good resources for general information:

The Council for Exceptional Children
Talented & Gifted Division (TAG)
1920 Association Drive
Reston, VA 22091
(Has a list of parent organizations)

The American Association for Gifted Children
15 Gramercy Park
New York, NY 10003

Mensa
1701 W. Third Street
Brooklyn, NY 11223
(Has a list of state coordinators)

The National Association for Gifted Children
Business Office: Dept. P. 2070
               County Road H
               St. Paul, MN 55120
Subscription to *The Gifted Child Quarterly*
               217 Gregory Dr.
               Hot Springs, AR 71901

National/State Leadership Training Institute
for Gifted and Talented
1255 Portland Place
Boulder, CO 80302
or
316 W. Second St.
Los Angeles, CA 90012

Gifted Children's Newsletter
530 University Ave.
Palo Alto, CA 94301

Association for Gifted and Talented Students
1627 Frankfort St.
New Orleans, LA 70122

Roeper Review
Roeper City & Country School
2190 N. Woodward
Bloomfield Hills, MI 48013

Resources for the Gifted
3421 N. 44th St.
Phoenix, AZ 85018 (Has free catalog)

TESTS NEVER LIE?

No issue has been more hotly debated by scholars, parents and fools than has the relevance of standardized group testing programs. Yet this remains as the primary, bona fide, official, certifiable evaluation of our children.

While the identification of preschool GCs depends almost entirely upon the observations of family members and independent testing/counseling professionals, the overwhelming majority of GCs are formally identified in the public or private school system. Because educators have been willingly cast in the role of intelligence evaluators, I think parents have a right to expect them to do a competent job. Unfortunately, it doesn't always work.

I've read volumes on standardized testing. I've completed several graduate-level courses on tests and measurements. I've given test batteries to anxious students chewing on pencil erasers. I've sat with parents and tried to explain that "test scores are only an indication of achievement" and "they don't mean everything"—all the while trying to ignore the reality that three adult strangers had come together at 2:00 in the afternoon to discuss them. And yet, I still can't get it all straight. I suspect that few classroom teachers and counselors fully understand the statistical ramifications of standardized scores. I know even fewer parents do.

Oh, we all know what we've been told:

1. An individual's scores vary from test to test.
2. There is such a thing as test sophistication.
3. Ten to fifteen points should be added to or subtracted from each raw score to create a range effect.
4. Tests measure only how well a student is adapting to a given school system. According to Leon J. Kamin, "The existing IQ tests, as they were designed to do, predict on a better than chance basis who will do well in the kinds of school training programs we now employ."[26] (Please note for future reference, the words "better than chance.")

And yet, *there they are*—those indelible two or three numbers. By their mere existence, they communicate a ranking. I don't care what the test experts continue to say: a teacher or a parent looking at a child's permanent school record thinks that an IQ of 130 is smarter than one of 120.

Those standardized group tests most often given GCs are Intelligence Quotient (IQ), achievement and reading readiness.

Do They Still Use the IQ?

In a word, yes. To this very day, nothing strikes fear to the heart like the IQ score. If you say it very quickly, it even seems reasonable: the mental age divided by the chronological age, multiplied by 100 (so the counselors don't get confused by decimal points). The "IQ" part is kind of cute and slangy, like IBM or PJ. The "score" part puts it in perspective—a win or a loss, as in the Super Bowl. It amazes me how we continue to say those numbers as if they were Holy Scripture written in the sky. It's as if we were all born with a set of individual fingerprints, a totally unique voice pattern and an IQ tattooed on every brain cell. Each day hundreds of thousands of people spend their professional lives trying to unlock the clues to all of our little brain tattoos. It is a fairytale come to life. There are social scientists, mathematicians, psychologists, psychometrists, counselors, computer technologists, salespersons, coveys of clerks and upper level managers, all working in the standardized testing industry. It must be gospel—it comes back from California on a computer printout.

Perhaps one of the most comprehensive investigations into the current mystique of the IQ was conducted by Evelyn Sharp in her book, *The IQ Cult.* (This should be required reading for any parent whose child has ever been given an IQ label.)

In it she says, "The public image of IQ testing—fostered by the solemnity and awesomeness with which early practitioners cloaked the process, handed down their findings like judgements from on high—is veiled in layers of myth, folklore and misconception. . . . To sum up, IQ tests were oversold in the beginning and capabilities were attributed to them that they never had."[27]

As with many things that get out of hand, the standardized group IQ test was born in a rather sensible manner. Early in the century, a psychologist (Alfred Binet) and a physician (Theodore Simon) constructed the first standardized test of intellectual functioning. Given individually, the purpose of the test was to differentiate those children who were unable to perform simple mental functions from those who were simply lazy or apathetic. Those initial tests consisted of tasks such as repeating digits, naming objects, and comparing the lengths of lines.[28]

Then came World War I. Before they could all sing "Mademoiselle from Armentières," things must have been rather frantic. Army recruiting officers hurried to screen, label and assign hundreds of thousands of fighting men and boys. Some enterprising soul came upon the idea of testing a lot of people at once (it makes sense, saves time and seems efficient), and we've been stuck with it ever since.

Primarily the IQ is a global assessment that does not discriminate abilities in specific content areas. (That little number is supposedly left up to the standardized achievement test.) IQ tests purport to measure language reasoning, memory, conceptual intelligence, social intelligence, numerical reasoning and visual skills.[29] Questions incorporated into the tests are constructed from teacher comments about the way in which students "appear" to be successful in school, and purchased from creative college professors.

There is a line of reasoning among many educators that the primary purpose of any test is to help a student and teacher recognize what the student does not know and needs to learn. The IQ test is based upon an attempt to capture what a student knows for certain. (Well, yes, guesses do count.)

And then there's that cloak of secrecy bit. Test distribution is meticulously controlled by test publishers. We're talking big bucks here. Giving our children standardized tests is a billion-dollar business. We're told that more people have the recipe for the Colonel's chicken than peek at an IQ test: "Distributors of tests try to restrict sales to qualified persons, just as the sale of medicine is restricted."[30] You have to prove you're somebody just to buy one. It is the self-imposed ethical responsibility of the test publisher to investigate the credibility of the purchasers' skills in proper test procedures. Of course, there are a few slipups.

College scholarships, federal funding and the pride of the school district can all ride on the crest of high standardized test scores. And whenever there is something big at stake, we seem to delight in "refining the system."

"Teaching to the test" is a logical and even admirably creative example of this skill. Oh, it's officially frowned upon, you understand. But if a fifth-grade teacher notices that a particular type of math problem is not covered in the administration's curriculum plan, and if she remembers that the achievement tests given to last year's fifth-graders had several examples of this skill—well then, she's only being responsible if she includes an extra math unit before spring testing. An English teacher can hardly be faulted if he knows that sophomore IQ tests rely heavily upon synonym/antonym word games. But it may never have occurred to you that your child can be cut out of the herd because some other teacher was not so good at heads-up ball-playing.

Some communities, disgruntled over plummeting academic results, have even discussed linking teacher salaries and benefits to standardized test scores. That could set off a test espionage network rivaling the OSS.

Many research projects (most notably, those conducted at Johns Hopkins University) have shown that without the careful, professional analysis of its subtest components, the IQ score can have little or no relationship to a child's real capabilities for learning. Each test manufacturer provides individual test scores and interpretation. Thus a superior ranking on one test could easily be interpreted as a high average ranking on another. Analyzing these tests and interpreting the results as they relate to each specific child is not easy. I have no blanket respect for anything and that most certainly includes Ph.D. psychologists and Ed.D. tests-and-measurements specialists. But basic common sense tells me they have at least had more sophisticated exposure to standardized tests than have teachers and counselors with expertise in other fields. And yet, in most public and private school systems, the classroom teacher does not have the luxury of such analysis. He or she is simply given a number. You may assume that classroom teachers learn "all about" tests in college. Few do; and even they often forget after their own final exams.

If you were asked to name the average IQ score, chances are you would say "somewhere around 100." This is generally true. And its widespread acceptance as truth is an interesting testament to the American public school system, the power of the press and the tenacity of folklore. Almost any literate adult in this country can recall being told by someone or having read somewhere that the average IQ is "somewhere around 100." It has been repeated countless times and reprinted in millions of high school and college textbooks. This image has been implanted in our collective psyche and it endures with timeless accuracy like a parable from the Old Testament.

In 1937, Terman and Merrill published the following IQ distribution scores and accompanying value labels for the Stanford-Binet Intelligence Scale:[31]

IQ	CLASSIFICATION
160–169	
150–159	Very superior
140–149	
130–139	Superior
120–129	
110–119	High average
100–109	Normal or average
90–99	
80–89	Low average
70–79	Borderline defective
60–69	
50–59	Mentally
40–49	defective
30–39	

So sacred is this image of IQ that every subsequent test distribution miraculously falls near its magical numbers. The average IQ on any other test is never 300 or 0.75, but always "somewhere around 100."

When Terman and Merrill updated earlier test score values (1973) they again reinforced their old labels. (That is sort of like Moses coming back to glance at the tablets and remarking, "Yeah, that's what He said, all right.") They concluded, "Here as before, an IQ of 100 will represent the performance of the average child at that age. An IQ of 116 represents performance one standard deviation above average or at about the 84th percentile of his age group, while an IQ of 84 falls one standard deviation below average. Thus, the historical meaning of IQ values is maintained...."[32]

I can read your mind. What's a cubit? Or rather, what's a standard deviation? SD (as we call it in the trade) is a way of comparing the scores of one group to those of another group. Both groups may have the same average score (mean) but a very different point spread. The comparison of point spreads is the standard deviation.

Time to Name Names

The Stanford-Binet (children) and Weschler-Bellevue (adults) are used primarily in clinical settings. Those standardized tests of mental ability most often used in schools are:

> California Test of Mental Maturity
> Cooperative School and College Ability Tests
> The Lorge-Thorndike Intelligence Tests (Verbal and Non-verbal batteries)
> Otis Quick-Scoring Mental Ability Tests
> American College Testing Program

Tests in Print is a compendium of over 3000 tests available for purchase. In it you can find details about the tests that will be given to your child. I would also suggest you consult *Psychological Testing* (4th edition) by Anne Anastasi. A professor of psychology at Fordham University, Anastasi combines the major principles of test construction with specific application guidelines. If you really feel up to the test yourself, you can attack a recent volume of the *Mental Measurements Yearbook,* edited by Oscar Buros. It contains synopses and reviews of current tests, a test publishers index and details such as the where, by whom and how much of test administration.

Achievement Tests,
or How Smart is Smart?

If an intelligence test were to measure the capacity of a drinking glass, then the achievement test is supposed to measure the water level.

Until the nineteenth century, the assessment of scholarship was a very personal matter. A student would discuss concepts and conclusions with teachers. In Greece, Socrates developed the art of academic dialogue. On the Kansas prairies the schoolmarm lined up her pupils and asked them to tell her what they knew. Up at Cambridge, scholars were given "orals" by a master of a specific subject.

Now in the computer society of the 1980s, these methods

seem old-fashioned, not scientific enough, not big enough. It isn't enough that a student understands all that she needs or wants to know of a specific subject. How much does she know compared to everyone else? Well yes, he's bright, but how many footcandles? Education—and American public education in particular—is in the big leagues now. We don't have time to assess individually and work with each student.

There's only one way to accomplish this Herculean task. Ask a large number of students (each on the same academic grade level) a series of standardized questions. Then compute their scores and get a ranking order. Any other student taking the same test can then be fitted into the peghole. It's called a percentile. If a student scores in the 87th percentile, it means that he scored higher than 86 percent of the thousands of students (same age, same grade level) who also took the same test. (Some achievement and aptitude tests are based upon a stanine—a composite scale of 1–9 points.)

Sounds scientific, doesn't it? But on some standardized achievement tests, a score in the 87th percentile can be separated by a score in the 64th percentile by only *two* multiple-choice questions. Your (Jason, Leon, Amy Lou) could have made a faulty erasure (machines won't score pencil marks that go outside the spaces on the answer sheet) and been fooled by a "distractor" (or trick answer). The result could have knocked out any chance for a scholarship, admission to a gifted junior high program or admittance into one of "the best" private kindergartens.

Many test opponents charge that the achievement test merely measures trivia. The 300 or so items on a single test, they contend, can hardly be representative of eleven or twelve years of diversified study.

In the *Test of Economic Understanding,* a subject area assessment for high school students, we find one such example:

Americans are a mixed-up people with no sense of ethical values. Everyone knows that baseball is far less necessary than food and steel, yet they pay ball players a lot more than farmers and steelworkers. Why?

a. Ball players are really entertainers rather than producers.
b. Ball players are more skilled than persons who get less pay.
c. Excellent baseball players are scarcer relative to the demand for their services.
d. There are fewer professional ball players than farmers or steel-workers.[33]

The reasons why a baseball player earns more than a farmer may constitute an interesting conversation during the seventh-inning stretch. It may even come up as they listen to the ball scores down at the Grange—but would you like your admission to an ivy league school of economics to be based upon your choice of a, b, c or d?

How Can They Test a Baby?
Preschool Tests and Measurements

Testing the intelligence and achievement of a child under the age of three is a very tricky business. It is during these first years that the brain undergoes its most rapid and dramatic physical development. The human computer system is constantly gathering, assimilating and responding to multifaceted stimuli. Every sight, sound, tactile sensation, smell and taste is being recorded as a foundation block for what we call intelligence and achievement. Assessing the parameters of this process is immediately complicated by four clear obstacles:

1. *Maintaining the child's attention.* It is virtually impossible to fully explain the testing rationale to even the most gifted three-year-old. In a word—he doesn't care. How can you justify the seemingly endless (and possibly boring) questioning? After identifying three or four pictures, or stacking a couple of blocks, a child of this age is just as likely to focus complete attention upon how well the blocks may bounce. Remember, *every* situation is a learning situation and satisfying her curiosity may be as important to the child as is answering the questions of a stranger.

2. *The limitations of the test administrators.* The success or failure of the test itself (validity) rests in great measure upon the skills of the test administrator. How skillful is this person in keeping the attention of the child? How skillfully can he inter-

pret responses that may be intermingled with random information?

For example:

TESTER: Lori, do you know where milk comes from?

LORI: Milk comes from the refrigerator, 'cause my mommy says we have to keep it cold even though the cow doesn't need to. Our refrigerator's green and has two doors.

Does Lori know that milk comes from mammals and most often a cow?

3. *The basic construction of most standardized tests.* Those standardized tests that claim to be most accurate in measuring intelligence and/or achievement (as based upon later tests) rely upon adaptation of known data to novel ideas. These abstract thought processes may allow a child to select a synonym or discern the difference between two geometric patterns. But most preschool tests rely upon skills that a child must already have been taught—that is, point to the doll's mouth, point to the red square, circle the dog, etc.

4. *Emotional handicaps.* Very often, the young child is traumatized by the testing situation. Insecurity with the new environment, fear of a stranger and anxiety transferred from a parent can drastically alter "performance" and test conclusions.

I remember Michelle. I met her mother while Michelle and several other five-year-olds were being evaluated for a gifted kindergarten program. "I just know Michelle is going to be terrified," the mother told me as she lit another cigarette. "She understands how important it is for her to do well today, but I just don't know . . . she may freeze up. I can't stand this waiting!" I learned from the school psychologist that during the entire fifty-minute evaluation, Michelle stood by the door and cried for her mother.

Tests for infants and young children have one of two goals: (1) a gross determination of physical and intellectual development, or (2) a prediction of success in school skills. All tests for young children are most accurate in identifying those children who consistently achieve below developmental milestones.

Some of the more widely used tests are the following:

1. *The Catell Scale.*
2. *The Gesell Schedule.*

These scales are most often the measurement used in a routine pediatric examination. They represent a cross section of motor and intellectual activities attributed to normal babies. According to the Catell Scale, for example, a normal six-month-old should be able to acknowledge and "regard" a cube, and follow with the eyes a ring in a circular motion.

3. *The Bayley Mental and Motor Scale of Infant Development.* This instrument appraises a child's attention, adaptive behavior and coordination. At six months, a normal child should:

Exhibit sustained inspection of a ring
Turn to observe a moving spoon
Vocalize displeasure
Smile at own image in a mirror

Other milestones include:

At 9.4 months: on command, puts cube in cup.
At 14 months: scribbles spontaneously.
At 17.8 months: follows directions using doll (e.g., "Point to the doll's eyes").

4. *The Kindergarten Evaluation of Learning Potential (KELP).* This test involves the teacher's evaluation of how a child responds to simple instructions such as building with blocks, interpreting signs, printing letters, etc. The most obvious problem for the young GC is that the test begins by underestimating skill levels. After several minutes of stacking blocks, a GC can become bored. A GC who is reading quickly tires of identifying letters and geometric shapes. Responses can then become passive and avoiding ("I'm tired") or active and aggressive ("I already told you that"). Either can result in a "low" score.

5. *The Boehm Test of Basic Concepts.* This test is supposedly an inventory of concepts needed for completing school work. Test items (that's what they call questions) relate to either space, quantity, time or miscellaneous concepts. For example: the child is shown a picture of three boys entering a school building. The child is asked to identify the boy nearest the school. In a picture with one adult and four children, the child is asked to identify the student who is third from the adult. The major problem with the Boehm test is that the multiple-choice format allows for too much random error. Like the KELP, it also underestimates the skill level of the child. The GC will often tire of the routine and draw lines through all choices, scribble in the margins or overintellectualize choices. The Test of Basic Experience also uses this format, but it is organized around school subjects.

6. *The Goodenough-Harris (G-H) Drawing Test (Draw-A-Man).* The G-H appears simple: the child is asked to draw himself. But the scoring is very complicated and subject to interpretation. The test administrator/scorer is given an illustrated guide including the point evaluation for details and accuracy of structure, features, clothing, etc. This is an easy test for parents to alter. Simply teach your child how to draw a boy or girl (appropriateness counts). Arms attached at real shoulders are quite a plus. Eyelashes run up the score and fingers count more than do club hands. (The test is more valid for the child with retarded mental abilities.)

The G-H test has another serious pitfall. Its surface simplicity makes it a favorite of amateur psychologists. Over-interpretation and -analysis can, for example, find severe emotional trauma and parental hatred ("Look at those heavily violent facial features") when the villain may really be a ball-point pen with erratic ink-flow.

A GC can be easily misdiagnosed by the Draw-A-Man test. He can be (1) retarded in fine motor skills (a common characteristic), (2) bored with drawing details at that particular moment, (3) just plain lazy when it comes to tasks for which he sees no purpose, or (4) all of these.

When Scott was being tested for admission to a gifted preschool, the psychologist handed him a blank sheet of paper and told him to draw a man. Scott looked at the paper and replied, "You can draw a man if you want, but I'm going to draw a robot."

I once asked Jessica (age six) why she didn't put faces on her family of stick fingers. "Don't need to," was her answer. "I know what they look like."

7. *The Peabody Picture Vocabulary Test.* In the hands of a skilled administrator, this test appears to be rather accurate (when compared to standardized tests given in later years). The administrator says a word and the child is asked to point to the appropriate item. In a series consisting of an apple, a cat, a butterfly and a star, for example, the child may be asked to identify the apple. It does tend toward cultural bias and is most successful with the child who has had a great variety of real-life experiences.

8. *The Metropolitan Readiness Test.* This test consists of two levels, one for the early part of the kindergarten experience and a second for the period between kindergarten and grade 1. Like most readiness tests, it tries to identify abilities needed for learning to read and following classroom instructions.

Finding patterns is one skill represented in Level II. For example, the child could be shown:

The test administrator will ask the child to look at the letters in the colored box (first box) and mark the group of letters that has somewhere in it exactly what is in the colored box. Before the test, the child is taught to mark the paper by drawing a line from one black corner to another: ◣◥ . An interesting dilemma arises here. If the test is computer-scored, a correct answer marked in an incorrect manner will be counted as incorrect: ◣◣ or ◥◥ . If the test is scored by a teacher or counselor, does that person adhere to the concept that part of the test is the ability to follow directions? Which is more important, identifying the truth, or identifying the truth in the prescribed terminology? Reason tells us that the former should be sufficient. Reality tells us that a kid who can't do "exactly what the teacher says" can often get the educational shaft. (Keep this concept in mind when reading the chapter on selecting an educational system for your GC.)

It's Not Just Fun and Games

The appropriateness with which a single test is applied varies dramatically. For example, in some school systems, forms of the Gesell (the scale of gross and fine motor development) are used to determine how children move through the established readiness program: held back in senior kindergarten, moved from junior kindergarten to senior kindergarten, moved to the first grade, etc.

This practice often provides unbelievable trauma for the parents of a GC. They may have been sailing along for a few years. Perhaps they've just accepted the fact that their kid is a GC. They've observed astonishing levels of verbalization, logic, memory and analysis. Suddenly someone tells them that their kid flunked kindergarten. (Nobody will use that phrase, but I guarantee this is what most parents will hear.)

The educators aren't sadists. There is an intense school of thought that if a child is "overplaced" in a grade level before all developmental skills are established, he will fail. Teachers don't like to see kids fail, so they're only doing what they think is best.

Measurements like the Gesell are based upon the motor developments observed in a large number of children at specific age levels. The gross and fine motor skills of many GCs are behind those of their chronological peers. (Obviously this doesn't include children gifted and talented in athletics or the fine arts. They can sail through the Gesell.)

There are lots of theories; here are two big ones:

1. GCs accelerate past these developmental stages before parents think to attend to their needs. (How many parents spot the precise period when a gifted infant needs to exercise those tiny finger muscles?) Therefore, they find it difficult or impos-

sible to go back to these developmental levels (remember Piaget) when their chronological time rolls around (usually in kindergarten).

2. GCs have thoughts and conceptualizations far advanced of their physical growth stages. (It's hard to write down that great poem you've created when you can't even color within the lines yet.)

Finally, what about the parents who don't give a toad's toenail if their kid accomplishes proficiency in penmanship? They can tell you that by the year 2000 we'll all be typing into computer terminals and that like calligraphy, cursive writing will become an ancient art form. What about the intelligent, successful and highly functional parents who themselves bump into the furniture? They can tell you that delayed gross motor skills don't matter to them—nobody in their family plays ball anyway. In fact, there are many accomplished adults on this very planet who cannot walk a balance beam, skip or write a straight sentence on unlined paper.

Everyone involved with gifted education seems to disagree on what to do about it.

Sally's parents held her in kindergarten for a second year even though she read on the third-grade level and understood fourth-grade math. She could not cut and paste with the skill of a normal three-year-old—the Gesell said so. Her parents did not want her to fail in a first grade filled with written assignments and tests.

Another set of parents (she holds a Ph.D. in tests and measurements) totally disagrees with the concept. "We have three GCs," she told me. "Two are in graduate school on research fellowships. They couldn't tie their shoes well until they were at least nine. They read before they could ride two-wheel bicycles. They all 'failed' the Gesell. I think it's a bunch of rot."

It seems to come down to one of those individual battlegrounds and a parable about doing what's best for each child. The point is, don't be buffaloed by these tests. I am personally aware of one school system that gave its teachers specific written instructions on how to handle typical parental reactions to the Gesell results. They concluded by advising teachers to "sacrifice the success probability of an individual student" rather than fuel the destructive potential of verbal, negative parents.

These testing situations are not the minor leagues, folks. You've got to play heads-up!

And It Gets Worse

Every schoolday, IQ and achievement scores are ritualistically recorded in tiny little boxes on seemingly ordinary manila folders—the permanent school records. I don't know of any study to verify this, but I suspect that a very high percentage of those eyes looking at your child's permanent record will instinctively glance at these numbers before reading anything else. And I'm certainly not the only one to have noticed. The participants in a cooperative research project in association with the University of Pittsburgh reported: ". . . we would predict that teachers having access to test scores would tend to rate students in terms of their objective scores. . . . This might result in an overconformance of grades to standardized ability measures. . . ."[34]

They call it the "Halo Effect." If teachers think that Little Mary Sunshine is smart (high IQ, must be smart), she will be questioned as one would question a smart child; she will be answered as one would answer a smart child, and she will be graded as one would grade a smart child. And God protect Lucy Low Score.

It doesn't take much imagination to see how the IQ and achievement scores can be adversely affected by outside circumstances.

1. Janie scored below her potential because she's a member of the inner-city hockey team, and they practiced for three hours the night before the test.
2. Sarah was coming down with the chicken pox.
3. Curt and David were busily attacking one another with silent laser guns instead of attending to the test.
4. Alex decided the whole thing was a bore.

One sunny morning I was forced to give 537 eighth-graders the California Test of Mental Maturity in the only room large enough to hold them all—the school cafeteria. They chugged their little brains out over the sounds and smells of the kitchen staff making a repast of fried pork chops, green salad, whipped potatoes and applesauce cake. I still can't look a pork chop square in the face without wondering how many teachers, scholarship committees and college admissions officers mulled over the numbers hatched that day.

Arlene Silberman very succinctly questions the reliability of standardized group testing in the article, "Tests—Are They Fair to Your Child?":

> How can IQ scores have meaning (except to label and classify) when neither psychologists nor educators agree on a definition of intelligence in the first place? How can achievement test scores have meaning when the tests measure only those parts of the curriculum that the test-makers consider important and, even more significant, only parts that can be fitted into the narrow computer-gradable format? How can reading-readiness scores have meaning when reading experts are still debating what skills are necessary for beginning readers?[35]

For years teachers and counselors have recognized the handicaps inflicted upon any child with special learning disabilities. For instance, a bright mathematics student with limited reading ability can score disproportionately low on math sub-tests if most of the questions are "story problems." "Farmer Brown had five cows and seventeen chickens. How many animals did he have if he sold one cow at market and ate two chickens for Sunday dinner?"

You Thought That Was Worse

As horrible as the standardized group tests can be for all children, they can be even more detrimental to the GC.

In a 1971 report to Congress, the U.S. Office of Education concluded that "as many as 50% of all gifted children may go unidentified if group tests alone are used."[36]

Individual testing can more accurately identify gifted students because the discrepancy between group and individual scores increases in direct proportion to levels of intelligence. In

English that means that more above-average students (scholarship, achievement) score below their actual achievement levels when tested in group situations.

James Alvino and Jerome Wieler addressed this problem in a recent issue of *Phi Delta Kappan* (a professional education journal). All standardized tests discriminate against the gifted. The main culprits, they say, are IQ tests and achievement tests.

The IQ test measures only a maximum of eight mental operations. Meanwhile educational psychologists point to the Guilford Structure of the Intellect Model in which it is hypothesized that human thought processes consist of over 120 mental functions. One researcher concluded, "Like no other present day label, the IQ scores continues to bask in a socially ascribed mystique. This tends to mask the blatant fact that the testing industry has not kept pace with the advances of educational psychology."[37]

Achievement tests are usually used in conjunction with the IQ test. A student achieves as expected, overachieves or underachieves. These tests are primarily based upon convergent thinking (focusing on a single solution): pick the best or most-often-correct answer. This concentration upon convergent thinking often eludes the gifted and creative child who is particularly skillful in divergent thinking.

Silberman reports of a gifted math student who "failed" to score his actual ability level on a standardized group achievement test. The young scholar reached a question asking for a skill he had yet to be taught—adding fractions of uncommon denominators. Forgetting the always-recited admonishments not to "dwell on a problem when you don't know the answer" (time is ticking away, you know), he was fascinated by this new mathematical concept. In the margins of his test paper, he drew little boxes representing the fractions and logically deduced the correct procedure and the correct answer. According to the official record, he had only answered five questions. Imagine the surprise of the teacher should this GC wind up in remedial math. For a more chilling thought, imagine the consequences should he be slightly passive and greatly ignored in remedial math.

Because of time and logistics, all group tests are built upon the multiple-choice question. Converging upon the psychometrist's (test maker/test grader) interpretation of what is the "best" or most "usually correct" answer "predetermines and stifles a child's thinking to the detriment of authentic discovery and/or creativity."[38]

If that weren't enough, one primary element in the multiple-choice question is the "distractor." This is the wrong answer that is close enough to the truth so as to be interpreted as correct. Its sole function is to distract the student.

You ask for proof. The California Achievement Test, Book 15C (fifth-grade level) includes some interesting examples:[39]

The student is asked to pick the word that is the same as the word in italics.

> *horrible* situation
> unusual
> exciting
> dreadful
> awkward

An awkward situation can be horrible to a child entering puberty and very aware of social presence. A dreadful situation can be horrible. But a timid child can also find an unusual situation unknown and thus horrible. And in the strict definition, the word exciting means to "arouse emotion" either positive or negative. A horrible situation can certainly evoke or excite to terror or even violence. *Funk & Wagnall's Standard Dictionary of the English Language* defines horrible as "exciting abhorrence; terrible." Dreadful is defined as "inspiring dread or awe; terrible." Seems to me that although the dictionary calls horrible "exciting" the best answer would be "terrible"!

> *select* the winner
> crown
> reward
> choose
> protect

Very often in this society, we reward the beautiful winner with a crown and then choose to protect her from the crowd. In

England, they choose to crown a king and then must protect his reward in the Tower. In a presidential primary, we choose the winner and instead of a crown, his reward is Secret Service protection.

> *inspect* the files
> sort
> open
> store
> examine

Now that you know what's in store, I'll let you openly examine and sort through this one for yourself.

The neat little package of IQ and achievement scores, Alvino and Wieler maintain, is mutually reinforcing the falsehoods of both. One predicts and the other stamps approval. They conclude that the only valid evaluators of a child's abilities are, and forever have been, the astute observations of an interested and innovative teacher.

But Just for the Record . . .

Okay, you hate standardized IQ and achievement tests—I mean, talk about your "elitist mechanisms to segregate the populace." But just what kinds of numbers are we talking about as entrance requirements to programs in gifted education, say in Anywhere, U.S.A.?

Every program sets its own selection standards, usually based upon a community definition of giftedness. The West Clermont Local School District of Amelia, Ohio, constructed a mathematical formula assigning values to three of four possible categories. Admission to the Special Program for Advanced Needs (SPAN) (everyone in education loves an acronym) is based on the following minimal requirements:

1. A group intelligence test score of 125
2. Scores on the California Achievement Battery of 90th percentile
3. Teacher nominations
4. Parent nominations

In the Washington Township School District, Indianapolis, children are selected for admission into the gifted education program based upon the following:

1. A six-month residence within the school system
2. One of the following:
   For intellectually gifted, an IQ score of 135 or better
   For academically gifted, achievement test scores of 8–9 stanine in at least six subject areas
   For creatively gifted, faculty evaluation based upon the Torrance Tests of Creativity
   For children gifted in the visual/performing arts, evaluation by a panel of professionals in the student's specialty area
3. Teacher nominations
4. Parent nominations

What Can You Do?

The standardized group testing industry has a very strong foothold in American education. New federal legislation aimed at diminishing cultural and sexual discrimination in testing promises to alter the path somewhat. BUT your GC may be a parent before the trend swings completely away from the current testing ritual. In the meantime, you can remember:

1. Don't abandon your own judgments. No one knows or cares about your child in quite the same way you do. Never trust a standardized test score over your own perceptions of your child's abilities and/or needs.

2. Educate yourself about the tests given your child. Go to the library and look up the individual tests in textbooks on educational psychology, tests and measurements or test statistics. Find out what even the experts hate about each test. Call or write the head of the School of Education at your state or local college/university. If you're persistent (and polite) someone on the faculty will be able to answer your questions.

3. Demand your right to information. You have a legal right to an explanation of any part of your child's education.

And this specifically includes test scores. You also have a right to a copy of your child's test (for a reasonable copying fee) *even* if the school has had the tests "machine scored" by a test publisher and must retrieve the tests of an entire class. Private schools are also bound by these procedures and are particularly attentive to subtle threats of public disclosure/discussion and gossip at the country club. Most importantly, if you believe that your child was significantly handicapped by a group testing situation, you can insist that she be retested individually.

4. Learn about the tests that *don't* discriminate against the gifted. Tests in divergent thinking—where there is no single correct answer—can (again, in the hands of an expert) be far more revealing about your GC's special abilities.

For example: The Torrance Tests (published by Personnel Press) are especially designed to measure creativity and include sections such as:

1. *Ask and Guess.* The student is shown a scene and asked to guess (create) what may have led to the scene and what might happen next.
2. *Product Improvement.* A toy is shown and the child is asked to suggest alternative uses for a commonplace object, such as a dish or lampshade.

In addition, the Remote Associates Test (RAT) asks the child to produce familiar but hard to retrieve verbal associations. Given the words, "blue, cottage, and rat" what familiar word can be associated with all three? The child is encouraged to use simile, rhyme or literary reference. The more answers, the greater degree of creativity.

Finally, aptitude tests for particular subjects can be more helpful for the child gifted in a single cognitive area.

5. Use parent power. It is *awesome.* Form a parent group to investigate the standardized tests in your school district. Why those specific tests? What will be done with the test results? Who on the faculty or staff will be in charge of the testing program? What is the experience level of the person or persons actually administering the tests? What alternatives are available?

How much does all of this cost? A school counselor can spend years begging a principal to stop using a specific test. An informed group of parents need only ask and it may never again see the light of day.

Notes

1. Sir Cyril Burt, *The Gifted Child,* Hodder and Stoughton, London, 1975.
2. Ruth A. Martinson, *Curriculum Enrichment for the Gifted in the Primary Grades,* Prentice-Hall, Englewood Cliffs, N.J., 1968.
3. Alfred L. Baldwin, "Piaget's Description of Development During Infancy," *Theories of Child Development,* Wiley, New York, 1967.
4. Herbert Ginsburg and Sylvia Opper, *Piaget's Theory of Intellectual Development: An Introduction,* Prentice-Hall, Englewood Cliffs, N.J., 1969.
5. For over seventeen years, Burton L. White and dozens of staff and faculty at Harvard University studied young children and the intricacies of the developmental theories of Piaget and others. The results of this labor are in the book *The First Three Years of Life* (Prentice-Hall, Englewood Cliffs, N.J., 1975). This account graphically illustrates the month-to-month development of the normal child.
6. T. G. R. Bower, *A Primer of Infant Development,* Freeman, San Francisco, 1977.
7. A. H. Maslow, *Motivation and Personality,* Harper & Bros., New York, 1954.
8. Sidney P. Marland, U.S. Commissioner of Education, Office of Education, in a report to the Congress, 1971.
9. Harold K. Hughes, "The Enhancement of Creativity," *The Journal of Creative Behavior,* 3:2, 1969.
10. James J. Gallagher, "Research Summary on Gifted Child Education," Department of Program Development for Gifted Children, Office of the Superintendent of Public Instruction, Springfield, Ill., 1966.
11. Joseph S. Renzulli, "What Makes Giftedness? Reexamining a Definition," *Phi Delta Kappan,* November 1978.

12. E. Paul Torrance, *Gifted Child in the Classroom,* Macmillan, New York, 1965.
13. Lewis M. Terman et al., *Genetic Studies of Genius,* vol. I: *Mental and Physical Traits of a Thousand Gifted Children,* Stanford University Press, Stanford, Calif., 1926.
14. Leta S. Hollingworth, *Children Above 180 IQ, Stanford-Binet Origin and Development,* World, Yonkers, N.Y., 1942.
15. Frankie H. Cooper, "The Gifted and Talented. A Descriptive Study of Parents' Perceptions of Preschoolers," unpublished thesis, Butler University, Indianapolis, 1979.
16. F. Laycock and J. S. Caylor, "Physiques of Gifted Children and Their Less Gifted Siblings," *Child Development,* vol. 35, 1964.
17. Gallagher, op. cit.
18. Lewis M. Terman, "The Discovery and Encouragement of Exceptional Talent," *American Psychologist,* 9:6, June 1954.
19. White, op. cit.
20. Halbert B. Robinson et al., "Early Identification and Intervention," *Gifted & Talented: Their Education & Development,* ed. A. Harry Passow, 78th Yearbook of the National Society for the Study of Education, Part 1, University of Chicago Press, Chicago, 1979.
21. Dorothy A. Sisk, "What If Your Child Is Gifted," *American Education,* 13:8, October 1977.
22. Charles Van Riper, *Speech Correction Principles and Methods,* 4th ed., Prentice-Hall, Englewood Cliffs, N.J., 1963.
23. Rita S. Dunn and Gary E. Price, "The Learning Style Characteristics of Gifted Children," *Gifted Child Quarterly,* 24:1, Winter 1980.
24. Benjamin Bloom, ed., *Taxonomy of Educational Objectives: The Classification of Educational Goals,* by a Committee of College and University Examiners, David McKay, New York, 1969.
25. Sisk, op. cit.
26. Leon J. Kamin, *The Science and Politics of I.Q.,* Lawrence Erlbaum, Potomac, Md., 1974.
27. Evelyn Sharp, *The IQ Cult,* Coward, McCann & Geoghegan, New York, 1972.
28. Leonard P. Ullman and Leonard Krasner, *A Psychological Approach to Abnormal Behavior,* Prentice-Hall, Englewood Cliffs, N.J., 1969.
29. Lee J. Cronbach, *Essentials of Psychological Testing,* 3d ed., Harper & Row, New York, 1970.
30. Ibid.
31. L. M. Terman and M. A. Merrill, *Measuring Intelligence,* Houghton Mifflin, Boston, 1937.
32. Lewis M. Terman and Maud A. Merrill, *Stanford-Binet Intelligence Scale Manual for the Third Revision,* Form L-M, Houghton Mifflin, Boston, 1973.

33. *Test of Economic Understanding,* Science Research Associates, Chicago.
34. Orville G. Brim, Jr., et al., "The Use of Standardized Ability Tests in American Secondary Schools and Their Impact on Students, Teachers and Administrators," a cooperative research project in association with the University of Pittsburgh, Pittsburgh, 1964.
35. Arlene Silberman, "Tests—Are They Fair to Your Child?" *Woman's Day,* November 1976.
36. Marland, op. cit.
37. James Alvino & Jerome Wieler, "How Standardized Testing Fails to Identify the Gifted and What Teachers Can Do About It," *Phi Delta Kappan,* 61:2, October 1979.
38. Ibid.
39. *California Achievement Tests,* Book 15C, CTB/McGraw-Hill, Monterey, Calif., 1977.

2

Coping with the News

After enough people tell you you have a gifted child, it must be so. You're pleased, of course—a few reservations, but pleased. Things could certainly be worse. Thank God she's normal. But your child is not normal. She's more than normal. Accepting the fact that you have a GC can be a threat to you and to all your beliefs about how things are supposed to "normally" function.

You flash back to high school, remembering the elite of your class, the football captain, prom queen and class president. The popular ones, the ones with straight teeth, most of them smart and on the Honor Roll: that would be wonderful for your child.

We are a society of winners and we reward only achievement. Most of us are trying to be the best, or trying to still be the best—at anything. It's unthinkable for a parent to urge a child on to mediocrity or failure.

Then you remember Weird Wilfred. He got straight A's, always won the science fair and his parents gave him a slide rule for Christmas. He mumbled when he spoke, wore sensible shoes and quoted Latin, for heaven's sake. Surely Weird Wilfred was an absolute genius.

Is that what it means to be gifted? Should you expect a child who daydreams about the relativity of matter? None of the prenatal classes or parent-to-be handbooks cover this sort of thing.

In talking with hundreds of parents whose children have been identified as gifted or unusually talented, I found that the news was very often mixed with fears and apprehensions. All sorts of old biases came to the surface as parents asked:

> Will my child be a social outcast?
> Can I cope with a child who can outsmart me?
> How can I find a school that will fully develop her talents?
> What do I tell other people? *Do* I tell other people?
> Should I try to find a few playmates and companions who are his developmental peers?
> Will this have a negative effect upon my normal children?
> Do her talents in some way belong to society?
> Do I have a responsibility to push him to reach his utmost intellectual capacity?
> Can I afford special tutoring or private schools?
> What would happen if I just did nothing?

The Story of One GC

We hadn't prepared for parenthood. We were through college and well into careers when this stranger suddenly came to live with us. Stuart spent his first twenty-five days in the Neo-Natal Intensive Care Unit of Norton-Children's Hospital. During that time, diagnoses ranged from minimal brain damage to hydrocephalus. We were told that his brain scan showed "atypical and erratic patterns." The doctors convened, conferred and concluded they didn't know what it all meant. It could be epilepsy—and then again, there had been observations of such irregularities in the brain scans of highly creative individuals.[1]

As a precaution, he was put on phenobarbital. Once administered, phenobarbital cannot be quickly withdrawn for fear of inducing seizure. The practice is to let the child "outgrow" the dosage. It was one year before we could discontinue the sedative.

It was his overaverage head circumference that was of most concern. The attending neurosurgeon insisted upon a regimen of weekly, monthly and then bimonthly visits. We rose and fell on every centimeter. Our only glint of hope in those days came from a dear old professor of pediatric medicine. One day, on the edge of my hearing range, he asked his students if anyone had ever bothered to see if "this child's parents simply have big heads." I often smiled at this as I dressed Stuart in those cute little baby outfits and folded away the matching caps that were always too small.

A correlation between overaverage head circumference and giftedness—particularly in the newborn—should not necessarily be inferred. A computer search of the international medical literature from 1970 to 1979 revealed only a few studies that even addressed this possibility. Children delivered at a Minneapolis hospital were monitored from birth until age seven. One observation was that "Larger head size from 1 year of age [until age 7] was . . . associated with superior intelligence."[2]

Another study involved measurements of the head circumferences of one-year-old children as they related to their levels of IQ at age four. "The 1 percent of children with largest heads at one year had 4-year IQ somewhat higher than children with head sizes at the mean, and a higher proportion of the largest-head children had IQ's of 120 or more at 4 years."[3]

Finally, a group of researchers in St. Louis compared the intelligence, reading achievement levels, physical size and social class of 360 boys of the same race aged 8–9½ years. Although the researchers were quick to point out that higher social class and parental occupation related to higher levels of every factor measured, they also stated that the ". . . mean IQ increases approximately 6 points with each increment of 1 cm in HC [head circumference] up to 54 cm with a leveling off at this point."[4]

All of these recent studies support the findings of Lewis Terman's classic 1926 study of the mental and physical traits of 1000 gifted children.[5]

After we brought Stuart home, we were told to expect learning disorders. Every day we watched every move he made. At that time, we decided we loved him—no questions, no expectations—we loved him for what he was. We never imagined he was gifted.

I noticed it when his developmental benchmarks were first a couple, and then several months ahead of those listed in my copy of Dr. Spock.

I made lists of his daily acccomplishments and presented them to our pediatrician as if to say, "See, he's normal—maybe a little ahead." I just assumed that baby books cited generalizations and that most children babbled syllables at three months, transferred objects from one hand to another at four months, and drank unassisted from a cup at five months. When he toddled up to the TV screen one day and read "Storm Watch," I stopped making the lists.

Three years later he was entertaining himself for hours with his almanacs and dictionaries; creating and reciting detailed narratives on the possible sequels to "Star Wars" and pounding out a reasonable piano rendition of "Heart and Soul." At that point, our parental goals took a turn.

For one thing, our book budget is ever expanding. I made early use of the public library, but Stuart became so involved with and possessive of each book that return dates were screaming nightmares. He understood the concept of borrowing, but books were something he consumed with obsession. He never could accept the fact that a book wasn't available for easy reference. And so his personal library grows. We compensate and buy books instead of "Turf Builder" or brand-name peas.

Much of the literature about GCs refers to a sense of order. Our GC lives in a rat's nest. He collects newspaper clippings, old greeting cards, candle remains, rocks and the lids to margarine tubs. He will go through the trash for interesting collectibles: an empty V-8 can or a toilet paper tube. He can account for every puzzle piece, Lego wheel and broken crayon. Discovery of one item missing leads to a frantic search and reunion with a like or contrasting object. I check for old food or anything that moves on its own, and try to stay calm.

GOING PUBLIC

Friends and Neighbors

I was surprised at the negative and sometime disapproving reactions I got from people when I first went public about our GC. I grew up in a time and place where "bragging" was a sin rivaling adultery or theft. I was also a participant in the great social drive toward honesty and self-disclosure that characterized the seventies. So, my comments were simply statements of fact (when appropriate to the conversation) or answers (when questioned).

"Does Stuart know the alphabet?"

"Yes, he's been reading for some time now."

"Did you know you have a very bright son?"

"Yes, he's gifted."

The reactions began to fall into patterns.

Disbelievers: "He's two and can read? Well, he's just memorized trademarks and key phrases. Besides, he's an only child and you probably work with him. With three, I don't have time for that. Did I ever tell you that all my children have perfect pitch?"

I could never grasp the inference. Did they mean that any child could be gifted if a parent would "work with him" or that had I not "worked" with mine, he would have perfect pitch?

Frankly I can't imagine not working with a child. We started early: encouraging infant babbling, reinforcing discovery by turning the house into a giant playpen and rewarding questions with answers. If any of that made a difference, well then, thank God we did it. Weeds thrive when tossed in the air and forgotten; children just hit the ground.

Curiosity seekers: "Hello, Stuart, your mother tells me you can read. What does this say, sweetheart?" while pushing a cereal box or a copy of *Redbook* under his nose.

Curiosity seekers would inevitably follow him around anticipating a quote from Longinus, a dissertation on the rights of man or at least an algebraic equation. My son always seemed to suck his thumb and pick his ears in front of these people.

Fans: "That's absolutely amazing! None of my kids could ever be that smart. You know, it's children like Stuart who'll someday find the cure for cancer and invent spaghetti that can't overcook. My (Betsy, Billy, LeRoy) could never do anything like that."

Of all the responses, this was the worst. I ended up feeling guilty because our son was himself.

Prophets: "Sure he can read now, but just wait until they get him in school! Then what will you do? He'll get bored and probably start smoking dope."

Actually, the prophets prey on a rather sad truth. Educators have estimated that children who have been identified as gifted and talented drop out of school at a rate from 3 to 5 times greater than do other students.[6]

School systems in general and public school systems in particular have a very poor track record when it comes to meeting the educational needs of the GC. A survey of national experts in the field of gifted education revealed that almost 90 percent believed that gifted programs at the primary grade level were either rare or nonexistent. Those gifted (or enrichment) programs identified by school administrators are most often a mere layering of somewhat advanced material onto an existing curriculum.[7] Even worse are the programs that equate gifted education with a doubling of simplistic assignments and/or homework.

The area of teacher education is equally grim. As of 1977, only twenty-one states had advanced degree programs in gifted education.[8]

A seven-year-old whose hobby is astronomy becomes bored in a science class where this subject is represented by a two-page poem on the rotation of the earth and moon. A third-grader who can explain the concept of square root loses interest when math becomes endless days and countless exercises in $4 \div 2 = ?$ and $8 \div 4 = ?$. No sane, literate adult would ever subject himself to even an hour of identifying "Bb for ball—the letter of the week." And yet a sane, literate six-year-old is expected to do just that. Demanding that a GC simply repeat the rites of educational passage makes as much sense as requiring an adult to practice writing her name 100 times before signing a check.

Finger Pointers: "A kid spends his whole life in school. Why can't you just relax and let him enjoy himself now? He'll learn how to read soon enough. Do you want him to turn into a bookworm? (Barry, Larry, Jerry) started to read and we just put him on 'hold' for a couple of years."

This line of reasoning truly escapes me. It is based on the belief that learning is painful and that a child's brain has a very limited tolerance. Too much, and the system explodes like a stuffed sausage. Moreover, suppressing a child's natural and intrinsic motivations for knowledge until an arbitrary time period is reminiscent of the old oriental practice of binding the feet.

"Pièce de Résistance": "Gifted children are adorable, and I would certainly never dream of kicking one; I just don't believe they deserve any special education. If they're so smart, they can pick it up for themselves."

You're absolutely correct if you picked up on the hostility. It's like the old joke about paranoia. "You're not paranoid, people really don't like you." When, for example, the parents of a GC stand up at a PTA meeting and ask for the recognition of their child's special learning problems, they literally may be told to "sit down and be grateful." When the parents of a GC speak of their child's day-to-day accomplishments or charming quotes or innocent observations of the ironies of life, no one really wants to hear. (And God forbid that the teachers label your child the offspring of a "pushy parent.") Why such hostility? Here are some of the reasons:

Gifted children are different. They threaten the concept of standardization and challenge the nongifted among us.

Gifted children evoke primordial fears of elitism. We all strive to be and to have the best. Yet, we somehow resent the fact that it may be inherently present in someone else. It's almost as if the gifted haven't "worked for it."

Gifted children are thought to come from predominantly affluent and/or privileged homes. The parents of such children could obviously afford quietly to provide special education for their prodigy. This simply isn't borne out by the facts. Socioeconomic indexes are not reliable predictors of giftedness. Rather, the research literature shows that more significant relationships exist between giftedness and family stability, parental emotional support and the educational backgrounds of parents. Many studies have testified to the cultural disadvantages "poor" children encounter when they are tested and/or evaluated by middle- to upper-middle-income educators, psychologists, etc. Or they may fail to be discovered or recorded because their parents cannot afford a $50 battery of intelligence tests.

Gifted children are independent and self-sufficient. The variety and intensities of their interests often isolate GCs from social situations. Yet they can be cooperative and contributing team members. Their personalities vary in accord with all the usual criteria. Some are witty and gregarious; some are sullen and aloof. In either case, their emotional and psychological needs are as acute as any child's.

Even more surprising was my reaction to the comments of others. I began to feel hesitant, no, actually apologetic for the fact that our child was gifted. "Well, yes, he can read the newspaper, but he doesn't know the multiplication tables and he can't do a thing with crayons."

I remember how we used to tease my father at the way he couldn't take a compliment. He had built much of our family house. But when guests would admire this nook or that cranny, he would fling open a closet, shine a flashlight to an uppermost corner and say, "It's really a sorry job. Can you see how that drywall doesn't meet?"

I was doing the same thing to our son: pointing up his shortcomings lest anyone interpret my talk of him as bragging; soft-pedaling the fact that at age four he functioned on the intellectual level of a seven-year-old; pretending that he too liked picture books, believed in Santa and thought that TV was magic. (On his fourth Christmas he told us that the story of Santa was absurd and he read about TV in *Popular Mechanics.*)

A parent of a GC is easily confused about his or her part in the matter. Did I really do something special in the genetic creation of this child? Did my choice of baby toys and selection of bedtime music make a difference? If so, should I be proud? Should I accept it with gracious humility? Should I actively protect him from the slings and arrows of outrageous neighbors? Should I, the "better creator," ease the discomforts of a "lesser creator"? I am, after all, such a grand person.

Most parents of GCs react to this confusion in one of two ways: (1) they become obsessed with the subject of genius; (2) they become obsessed with avoiding being obsessed with the subject of genius.

The former category contains the insufferable bores we all know and yawn to. I can't believe that anyone sets out to be a bragging bore of a parent. It must just happen (like scurvy). And it rarely has anything to do with the child.

People in the latter group seem driven by a fear of being seen as boastful parents. As a result, they make comments such as:

> "She really isn't gifted; she just catches on faster than other children."
> "I never use the word 'gifted.' It doesn't sound right."
> "We would never brag about our son. We wait for people to find out for themselves."

These comments disturb me. The first is a denial of fact and it reeks of self-deception. The second is as wrong as hiding a handicapped child in the cellar. The third is also deceptive, but in a far more calculated way. It seems to me that when the parent of a GC turns an avoidance of bragging into private gloating, exploitation is taking place. A child is being used to soothe and bolster an adult ego. I'd rather spend time with the bragging bores.

Humility can be an endearing personal trait. It seems to come across at its best when a winner gives recognition to all those who also played the game. But this kind of humility is artificial because it is based upon an assumption of superiority.

When you are the winner in a race, you are not humble when you say, "I'm really not that fast"; you are incorrect.

Gifted children are not intrinsically superior children. They are simply different. Such differences do not need to be defended by humility or cloaked in a modest, "Aw, shucks." This is because a difference becomes superiority only when it evolves into excellence. A GC who does not excel is not superior; any child who does excel, is.

Coping with It All

I believe each parent must establish a plan of action at this point:

1. Decide how you really feel about your child and take a stand. If you're proud—then say so. Haven't we all seen enough plays about children who long to learn of a parent's love and pride? If you're bound to and unhappy with a school system, become a militant within the Parent-Teacher Organization. If militancy doesn't fit you, forget about it and make creative use of the city zoo, libraries, 4-H, museums, public concerts, art fairs and television.

2. Seriously examine any tendencies you have to protect the "feelings" of other parents. I suspect that masking the abilities and talents of your GC is really the height of intellectual snobbery. If you can be big enough to accept their child as an intrinsically valuable human being, why can't you give other parents the same chance to accept your GC?

3. Concentrate on developing a strong sense of self-worth in your GC. If he is taunted by playmates for doing his math homework instead of watching the Super Bowl, go ahead and flex your values. Tell him you think knowing math is more important than knowing Terry Bradshaw's jersey number, and that it's okay for him to think so too. Children's literature can be a great help here. *The Monster in the Third Dresser Drawer and Other Stories* by Janice Lee Smith (Harper & Row) is a fun and sensitive tale about a boy who successfully avoids victimization.

4. Get busy with some of your own interests and goals, just to keep it all in perspective. You won't have time to stew over the probing questions of the scout leader if you're on your way to a photography class.

Some parents have no such conflict when going public. Andy's father was a case in point. He loved it.

At the zoo he would ask his five-year-old daughter, "Can you spell pachyderm?"

And Andy would oblige, always playing to the crowd.

A sort of game developed between them and it amused them both immensely.

In the bank lobby he would ask, "Andy, what's the name of this plant?"

A little voice would answer, *"Ficus benjamina,* Dad. That's a dracaena over there."

The proud father never missed an opportunity for her to read the menu and place her own order when the family ate in restaurants. (Andy's mother always felt uncomfortable with this and tried to look distracted or rearranged the silverware.)

Finding Playmates for the Two-Headed Kid

I started with a positive, absolute rule *never* to become involved in the squabbles my son would have with his friends. As a concept I still think it has merit. I've discovered weaknesses in the practice.

Very often, those specific behavioral traits that mark a GC can lead to peer conflict something akin to guerrilla warfare. Independence, intensity of concentration and nonconformity can become manifest as impatience, obstinance and severe "bratism."

As the parent of a GC you may hear aspersions such as these pour from the lips of your own sweet angel of a child:

"Don't scribble in my book, you barbarian."

"How am I supposed to understand you with that stupid thing in your mouth." (The reference was to a pacifier.)

"This is my room, so you get to play with whatever I give you."

"If you weren't so dumb you could figure it out for yourself."

Sometimes in groups of children with heterogeneous abilities, the GC can be a little tyrant, ordering everyone else about, demanding to be in charge and usually succeeding. I have heard parents' reactions that range from, "Yes, we're very concerned," to "So, what's wrong with that?"

I believe this tendency to ramrod through a group of chronological peers needs to be met head on. Try to schedule time when your GC can be with other GCs. This contact is important for several reasons:

1. Your GC needs to learn that his interests and abilities are not unique.
2. Your GC needs to have some peer relationships in which she also is stimulated.
3. Sometimes the "king of the mountain" needs to be challenged.

Sales Clerks and Other Strangers

I knew of a woman who pinned a sign to her daughter's T-shirt. It told the neighbors exactly where things stood: "Please Do Not Feed This Child." A similar sign for the GC would read: "Please Do Not Act Astonished at What I Can Do."

Unrealistic praise and doting can be detrimental to any child. Because the GC is usually more perceptive and responsive to adult attitudes, wide-eyed gaping at everything she says or does can be downright destructive. Everyone likes praise and a sincere compliment. But public scenes of adoration can be a little hard to handle, for both of you. A GC can easily turn into a junior Gestapo colonel or a miniature Milton Berle.

I was initiated very early in the game. One hectic afternoon I stopped in a furniture store to check an order.

As I discussed my concerns with the manager our GC (then age three) casually began reading aloud, "Five Days Only, Pre-Inventory Carpet Sale," "Thank You for Not Smoking," "Ask about Our Layaway Plan." It caught the attention of a passing consultant.

"What did you say, Honey?" she asked. My son obliged with a repeat performance.

"Look at this," she called to some customers.

An inventory clerk put down an ottoman and came to see what was happening. A crowd gathered and Stuart was placed atop a bamboo sofa table. People were going crazy: passing up magazines and sales slips, pointing to signs on the walls and labels on the merchandise. He read and they applauded. It looked like a scene from an old Shirley Temple movie. Only Bill Robinson was missing. I made my way to him just as talk in the crowd turned to: "Can he write his name, too?"

This episode taught me one thing: be prepared when someone yells "Showtime" and your kid is the dancing bear.

A few helpful hints for avoiding public scenes:

1. Remain steadfast in the task at hand. Answer politely (or in a manner best representing your personality) and get on with it.
2. Give your child a few ego strokes and change the subject. "Yes, we're very proud of him. Did you give back my credit card?"
3. Briefly excuse yourself. "I'm sorry, but we have to get home before our Big Macs cool down."
4. Pick up your GC and leave.

EXAMINING YOUR RESPONSIBILITIES

To Your Child

I've heard a lot of educators speak about the responsibilities of rearing a GC, sort of a sacred call to gently nurture the saviors of the planet. Don't believe it. The phrase "gifted child" leaves the subtle but unmistakable implication that he is gifted first and a child second. Exactly the reverse is true. A five-year-old who can find the common denominator in a series of unlike fractions usually can't find a clean pair of underwear in his dresser drawer. A three-year-old who works the crossword puzzle probably still sleeps with a beloved stuffed friend. A particularly verbal ten-year-old may lack the experience to discern when she is being astute and when she is merely being an ass. A physically advanced four-year-old can sprint across a gymnastic balance beam, spring to the floor and tell you that she was trying to keep the sharks from biting her toes. Your first responsibility is to a child, not a gift. And don't ever forget it.

About being pushy: No one would ever challenge a parent who insists that a child daily brush his own teeth. It's considered a basic. And yet here is a truly pushy parent. Demanding that a child stop something that's fun and brush his teeth! And for what? Parental goals of personal hygiene? Some universal truism about plaque?

And yet if this same parent took the case to the school board, ten out of ten would probably say: "Tell your kid to brush his teeth. It's for his own good."

Apply this to giftedness.

Mark is musically gifted. His mother insists that he practice violin for one hour before playing ball or watching "Laverne and Shirley."

Susi is a fifth-grader and a mathematical genius. Her parents meet with the school principal and ask that she be allowed to take ninth-grade algebra.

Michelle is a six-year-old who reads Agatha Christie mysteries. Her parents ask the first-grade teacher for class reading material that transcends "Oh Sally, See Spot."

Bryan wants to be a veterinarian and reads all he can on the care of animals. His second-grade science book implies that only cows give milk. He objects in class, proceeds to discuss the mammary functions of all mammals and is scolded by the teacher. His parents explode.

Every parent has a responsibility to protect any child from situations involving undue stress. Parental responses are not necessarily pushy.

Sooner or later, your GC will notice that she is different. And as all children are prone to do, she will equate difference with personal failure. It's very easy for a child to think something's wrong when she doesn't have the same interests as her chronological peers. She will notice that adults take notice.

These are the most difficult days for the parent of a GC. What you must do is teach your child to value herself. Help your child to become self-actualized. This means providing early opportunities for personal decision making.

I had a friend who made a Superman suit for her six-year-old son. He loved it and wore it whenever he could. Once when the two of them were traveling, he wanted to wear his costume to the hotel's most elegant restaurant. He presented a reasonable case. Superman was his hero and had always been seen in positive terms. The costume was as grand to him as were his gray pants and navy blazer to his mother. The Superman suit, he reasoned, would in no way interfere with his dinner or his behavior that night. He undertood the difference between fantasy and reality; he just wanted to wear the suit. Faced with this logic, she decided that the only counterargument was her own possible embarrassment. They went to dinner—she in her evening gown, he in his Superman suit. They had a perfectly wonderful time.

Be honest, especially when you're wrong. Because they are so adept at observing and responding to adult behaviors, GCs are the first to pick up on your errors. You won't be able to fool them by changing the subject. Take the opportunity to teach them that the best way to handle mistakes is to learn from them.

Preserve your child's right to discipline. Every child deserves a parent. Those experienced in the education of GCs often stress their needs for order and structure. They have difficulty functioning in a chaotic, illogical environment. Know your facts, set your rules, explain your rationale and firmly hold your ground. The fact is that you're the parent, and she's the kid.

To Society

I remember being frightened during the seventh grade by a social studies lecture on the Soviet Union. The teacher told us that schoolchildren in Russia had to take a series of examinations designed to determine how they could best serve the state. They would have no choice in their future careers or goals. If the tests showed a child should be a doctor, off she went to medical school in Moscow. If the tests showed that a child should be a farmer, off he went to the fields of the Ukraine.

What if I took such tests and they destined me to life as an auto mechanic? I even had a nightmare about greasepits and valve jobs.

The same concept applies when we look upon our GCs as a natural resource or public domain. Some GCs simply won't want to spend their lives in study and/or research. Some won't bother with college. Some will turn to the crass and material pleasures of a transparent, plastic, disposable society. Some of them are just going to fail, and they have a right to do so.

Finally, never, never expect your GC to be gifted at all times in all things. He has a right to get a C in music appreciation when you know he's been playing Mozart since age five. She has a right not to go out for the chess team, despite the "honor of the school."

To Your Other Children

First and foremost, the siblings of a GC have an inalienable right to normalcy. Sometimes all children in a family are gifted. But it's not fair to anyone for a parent to expect this always to be the case. Demanding that one child live up to the accomplishments of another or that one child repress skills so as not to threaten the other can be the seeds of lifelong sibling hatred.

We know a couple who brought forth two daughters in eighteen months. The older daughter suffered minimal brain damage at birth, the younger was a GC. As the girls went through early development, the younger began to duplicate and then exceed the accomplishments of her older sister. The girls had reversed roles, and in the minds of the parents, this was wrong.

When the older daughter was held in the first grade for a second year, the parents delayed the enrollment of their GC. They feared the girls would end up in the same class.

At the end of the next school year, the parents were approached by the school principal and told that the GC (now the wonder of the kindergarten) needed to be working with the second-graders. They stood steadfast in the conviction that she not be allowed to surpass her older sister.

I remember a similar scenario in Shakespeare's *Taming of the Shrew*. The Minolas were desperate for Katherina, the older daughter, to marry. Only then could her younger sister do the same. On stage it seemed amusing that parents could be so obtuse.

To Yourself

Parents of GCs almost always describe themselves in one of the following ways:

"Oh, what miracle hath been wrought." Gifted children do not spring forth like mushrooms any more than do other children. Only adoptive parents have a legitimate right to claim they don't know how it happened. Such "hand wringers" and "homage payers" often take this stance in a not too subtle (be it ever so subconscious) attempt to escape the hard work ahead. If they had no responsibility in the creation of the GC, how could they possibly be expected to provide challenging educational experiences or emotional guidance?

"Who cares? I don't care." (Liar, liar, pants on fire.) I've never met a parent with this viewpoint who, upon further discussion, failed to change the tune. If for no other reason than vicarious ego-gratification, parenting a GC is an event that eludes apathy.

"I always knew I was one." Without question, most parents of GCs believe they are gifted adults. Few would use the word "genius," preferring instead to refer to themselves as: "intelligent," "rather bright," "creative," "an underachiever."

"Both Jim and I come from families where education is highly valued. It was always understood that we were to go to college and excel in every area. My brother and his wife also have a gifted child."

"We had our share of family geniuses. My father was a scholarship student at MIT and Mother is a law professor. My wife's uncle used to spend weeks at a time locked in his basement, working on all sorts of weird inventions."

"Yes, I would say that I was also what they now call gifted. But I was a real goof-off in school. I never cracked a book, but I could walk in cold and pass any test."

"I guess you could say Sheri's father was smart. He could always remember anything he read. I had to work harder, but I could usually get it sooner or later. I do seem to have some talent for music."

No matter how you define yourself, the task at hand is not an easy one. Your GC will require more time, more patience, more research and planning than will many children. He will consume knowledge as a Texan consumes barbeque. And you will be the one primarily responsible for satiating that appetite. He will question everything, especially your knowledge and authority. But keep your responsibilities in perspective. Your GC is still a separate entity; his successes and failures will be his own.

Take a break and relax. Some day you'll be searching your attic for things to fill his first apartment.

Notes

1. Creativity and intelligence are believed to require two different thought processes. The evaluation of either through brain waves is often dismissed in both medical and educational circles. However, one clinical psychologist from Harvard conducted an interesting study into the correlation of alpha waves and creativity. Using the electroencephalograph (EEG), he observed that ". . . creative people have higher resting levels of [alpha] brain wave activity when working on a problem" than do noncreative individuals. Colin Martindale, "How Excitement Fogs Imagination. What Makes Creative People Different," *Psychology Today*, 9:2, July 1975.
2. Robert Fisch et al., "Children with Superior Intelligence at 7 Years

of Age," *American Journal of Diseases of Children,* 130:5, May 1976.

3. K. B. Nelson and J. Deutschberger, "Head Size at One Year as a Predictor of Four-Year IQ," *Developmental Medicine and Child Neurology,* vol. 12, August 1970.

4. Warren A. Weinberg, M.D., et al., "Intelligence, Reading Achievement, Physical Size and Social Class," *The Journal of Pediatrics,* 85:4, 1974.

5. Lewis M. Terman et al., *Genetic Studies of Genius,* vol. I: *Mental and Physical Traits of a Thousand Gifted Children,* Stanford University Press, Stanford, Calif., 1926.

6. Gene Maeroff, "The Unfavored Gifted Few," *The New York Times Magazine,* Aug. 21, 1977.

7. Jeanne L. Delp and Ruth A. Martinson, *A Handbook for Parents of Gifted and Talented,* 2d ed., Ventura County Superintendent of Schools Office, Ventura, Calif., 1977.

8. *Ibid.*

3

Education,
Like Charity, Begins
at Home

Even if it's just you and the kid—your GC is part of a family.
And as you can well imagine, a lot of social scientists are intensely interested in the specific kind of a family that produces,
nurtures or doesn't squelch a GC.

Study into the home environments of some successful and
eminent members of society has revealed that these individuals
were most often identified early and given a "special position"
within the family structure. This means that the parents gave
special attention to the GC's talents and educational needs.
Moreover, this special position within the family most often
came about because the GC was (1) the oldest child, (2) the oldest son, or (3) the only son.* It is also common knowledge that

---

* I'll discuss this matter of male/female GC with greater detail in Chapter
4. Statistically, the evidence shows more males than females in gross account-
ings of GCs. With my final female breath, I will argue the validity of these
numbers. One study from the University of Michigan suggests that overall sex
differences occur because during adolescence, girls show more vulnerability to
a decline or a failure to continue acceleration in IQ. Since most gifted programs select participants during one or two adolescent periods, more boys
than girls are identified (Eleanor P. Hall, "Sex Differences in IQ Development

parental interests often dominate the achievements of GCs. Both points are illustrated as a researcher reminds us that Mozart's older, brilliantly academic sister was "shelved as soon as their musician father became aware of Mozart's (musical) talents."[1]

One need only look to the children respectively chosen for success by the Kennedys, Churchills, Roosevelts, etc. And when his basketball-coach father was told by the obstetrician that Marquis Johnson (College Player of the Year, 1976) would grow to be over 6½ feet tall, a basketball/developmental program was immediately designed and then initiated when the athlete was two years old.[2]

Empirically, statistically and researchly speaking, we have much data. Walter Barbe studied the family backgrounds of 456 GCs with IQs ranging from 120 to 164 and concluded:

1. The gifted child appears to be either an only child or first born in a family of two.

2. 87½ percent were reared by both parents.[3]

(Note: This twenty-five-year-old study may reflect trends in the general society, as well as in the families of GCs. In 1956, a larger percentage of children were reared by both parents than is the case now.)

Before you put your second and third born in a bag with the river-bound kittens, recent opinion is that more first-born and only children show up as GCs because they enjoy a relatively longer period of intense adult relationships.[4] Seems simple to me—spend equal amounts of time with numbers 2 and 3.

In another study, it was concluded that male GCs receive more parental encouragement to play with science-related toys than do female GCs, and that precocious students tended to come from "typical" middle-class families in which the mother was more achievement-oriented than was the father.[5]

In examining the "Differences in Parental Environment

and Correlated Variables for Intellectually Gifted Students," *DAI*, 39:2A, August 1978). The reasoning seems clear to me. Since females show equal (and in some cases, higher) levels of intellectual development before adolescence, too many of our young women must still think it's not so smart to be too smart.

Needed for Degree Achievement for Gifted Men and Women," questionnaires were randomly sent to 400 members of Mensa. "Warmth" from the opposite-sex-parent seemed particularly important for inspiring achievement among males, while females expressed the need for warmth from both parents.[6]

In a study of 114 children with Stanford-Binet scores in excess of 140, the parental education levels correlated substantially with both IQ and achievement scores of boys, while the education levels of parents correlated only with the achievement scores of girls. The researchers suggested that the boys were more responsive to environmental (family) factors than were the girls.[7] You can draw your own conclusions from these possibilities:

1. Boys are more persuasible?
2. Girls are more bull-headed and/or independent?
3. Parents try to influence boys more than they do girls?
4. Educated parents stress achievement, not intelligence, in girls?
5. Noneducated parents stress neither achievement nor intelligence in either girls or boys?
6. Something else altogether.

We've discussed the GCs studied at ten-year intervals by Lewis Terman. Another researcher reviewing "Sources of Life Satisfactions of the Terman Gifted Men" (at average age sixty-two) learned that:[8]

Occupational satisfaction and work persistence were predicted by feelings of satisfaction, ambition and good health at age thirty.

Family satisfaction and success in marriage (defined by positive responses on an attitude scale) were predicted by "good" childhood social adjustment and positive attitudes toward parents.

A study of GCs and "parental variables" conducted at the University of Michigan revealed the following:[9]

On creativity:

Mothers who value self-defense (that's what it said) and being affectionate, and fathers who value being considerate, have creative children.

Being rated as distractible and extroverted seemed to lessen the children's creativity.

Fathers who expressed high marital role tension had children who scored high on verbal originality. (Those kids probably heard more creative language at home.)

On achievement:

As a group, achieving children were perceived as being "introverted" by fathers and not extroverted by both parents. ("Not extroverted" is research jargon for "sort of introverted, but not really.")

Both parents rated achieving boys as introverted, while boys rated as extroverted by both parents did not achieve in arithmetic. (See, males also have their stereotypic crosses.)

Based on work by Robert Sears,[10] researchers describe all children as coming from three styles of living: authoritarian pattern, compromising pattern or chaotic pattern. The child models after his home environment and approaches other life experiences (namely school) with this basic viewpoint. Also significant are (1) the physical setting of the home and the availability of objects, and (2) the way routine child-rearing tasks are handled by parents (discipline and rewards). "The behavior origins of school success and a successful society are begun in the home."[11] (My mother always told me that.)

Speaking of mothers, researchers at the University of North Carolina concluded that "the major issue is, can one look within an apparently homogeneous social class group and predict the child's later intelligence from information about the child's mother? The answer from these data is clearly, yes."[12] They went on to state that the most significant factors in this prediction were the child's birth order and the mother's educational status.

A 1975 study entitled "Mothers of the Gifted" reported that

GC mothers are academic achievers: 47 percent held a bachelor's degree, 9 percent held a master's and 2 percent held a doctorate. (In 1970 statistics for the general female population were: 7.2 percent for bachelor's, 1.6 percent for master's and 0.1 percent for doctoral levels of education.)[13]

British female GCs who were high achieving students in both mathematics and French reported that they identified with their fathers more than with their mothers.[14]

Mothers of GCs living in the greater Los Angeles area were polled and reported:

Psychological ages younger than chronological ages. (Everybody in California says that!)
A low percentage of divorce.
Small families.
That they were themselves achievers.[15] (But then, non-achievers probably wouldn't have bothered to send back the questionnaire.)

Mothers of adolescents judged creative were found to stress a variety of experiences, enthusiasm and a democratic parenting style. Mothers of adolescents judged less creative stressed conformity, studiousness and socially appropriate behavior.[16]

Compared with mothers of average and overachieving males, "the mothers of under-achieving sons were more dominant, rigid and restrictive in the sense of being possessive and intrusive. Mothers of under-achieving daughters were more dominant, rigid and restrictive in terms of being protective."[17]

Psychologists have argued long and hard over whether or not the "democratic" parent was the "good" parent, and whether or not the "authoritarian" parent was the "bad" parent. A study reported in the *Journal of Clinical Psychology* found support for the theory that children who are high achievers (school grades) tend to be conforming, orderly, docile and conventional. These children reported the attitudes of their parents as being directive and unchallengeable. Sounds good, but what does that mean in English? "Directive" is a buzz

word of the social scientists. It means a statement or question
that does not facilitate choice or discussion. Examples of directive statements would be "Take out the trash," or "Did you
pass the math test?" Nondirective alternatives would be "I
really could use some help with the trash," or "Tell me about
your math test." The "unchallengeable" parent has a universal
credo for all situations: "I said no, and I meant it." Both attitudes usually impede parent/child communication. However,
back to our high achievers. Academic success is now seen as
only one single type of giftedness. Nevertheless, it doesn't take
much imagination to see that if a kid never challenges parental
authority, she will never challenge academic authority; she will
probably receive high marks.

"It was found that the mothers of high achievers were more
authoritarian and restrictive ... than the mothers of low
achievers." And "the parents of high achievers of gifted intelligence also seemed to have more punitive attitudes with respect
to child rearing."[18]

In an article directly following the one containing that pro-
nouncement:

"... the mothers of adult male schizophrenic patients em-
phasize conformity, conventionality and obedience ... in their
child-rearing methods." Furthermore, the mothers "... showed
an extremely domineering, smothering, close relationship with
the child. In group session very often they indicated where the
patient was to sit, what he should talk about and frequently
they chided him on his behavior."[19]

You could get schizophrenic yourself trying to decide which
expert has the proof as to the method most effective in rearing
a GC. From these studies (and hundreds more) we can deduce
that should you choose to be an authoritarian parent you take
your chances. Your GC could turn out to be a healthy, disci-
plined scholar or a "nervous wreck" of a valedictorian. Obviously, the "democratic" and "chaotic" parents run similar
risks. No guidelines, no rules, no discipline: these can also result
in catastrophe.

Psychologist Rudolph Schaffer says that it isn't as simple as
deciding what kind of parent you are because "... children are

just as capable of affecting parents, thus producing a much more complex picture of interaction."[20] He believes that the "trick" is to dovetail your behavior to that of the child's.

And for something to keep you awake tonight: In *Readings in Educational Psychology* we find, "Generally then, children who place human figures at a relatively large distance from one another have mothers who are depicted as angry and hostile."[21] (There will be a slight pause while every mother checks her kid's latest artwork.)

So what have we? If you are a male, first-born or only child of happy, educated, loving, middle-class parents who stay to-gether, pick the "lucky" parental style, support your school, provide you with extracurricular stimulation (including sci-ence-related toys) and show you lots of "warmth," you have a pretty good chance of being a high-achieving GC. It will also help if your mother is slightly (but not greatly) authoritarian and greatly (but not slightly) independent and/or your father "expresses high marital role tension." (You know, that phrase was never explained to my satisfaction.) So what else is new? If you didn't turn out to be a GC after all that help, you deserve to be stripped of your "Boy Genius" badge. But what about everybody else's kid? We have statistical evidence that GCs can evolve from any creative combination of cultural, environ-mental, financial and philosophical surroundings. They come out of everything except Cracker Jack. And a high percentage of eminent personalities suffered severe environmental trauma including the early loss of one or both parents.[22] So how can we really pinpoint rules of parenting that are sure to work?

HOW TO GET ONE
OR KEEP THE ONE YOU'VE GOT

As I began to write about the in-home education of GCs, I real-ized that I must have been drunk when I first agreed to do it. I mean, the audacity of trying to tell you how to grow your own GC is outrageous.

Most amazing is the fact that I am in no way a model mother. Anyone who knows me will vouch for that. I do not like most children's activities. (It has nothing to do with the children; I didn't like much of that stuff when I was a child myself.) I do not like sitting with the children at holiday dinners; I do not like bouncing strange babies capable of exuding from either end; I detest "cute" and "toothless slurring" and "runny noses." Every time I have to clean the soap scum off his bath toys I'm ready to give them and the kid to the Goodwill. I never remember to make the Kool-Aid. My point is that if I can help rear a GC, there's no question that anyone can. You just have to have a plan.

I'm not going to tell you how to plan activities for your GC such as going on field trips; playing games and puzzles (dragons or otherwise); collecting; keeping a journal; learning magic (GCs love magic—it's the only socially acceptable way of outsmarting people); joining the Scouts; creating codes; traipsing off to the planetarium, aquarium and any otherariums; going to plays, ballets and concerts; cutting and pasting; playing visual memory games (such as Concentration); rhyming; drawing pictures to story narration; developing gross motor skills; arting and crafting; gardening or playing poker. You probably know all of that by now; and if you don't, there are plenty of sources available:

Fredelle Maynard, Ph.D.
*Guiding Your Child to a More
Creative Life*, Doubleday,
New York, 1973

Brandon Sparkman and Ann Carmichael
Blueprint for a Brighter Child
McGraw-Hill, New York, 1975

Junior Girl Scout Handbook
Girl Scouts of America
830 Third Avenue, New York

Big Bird's Busy Book
Michael Frith and Sharon Lerner,
Random House/Children's Television
Workshop, New York, 1975

Herbert Kanigher
*Everyday Enrichment for Gifted
Children at Home and School,*
Ventura County Superintendent of
Schools Office, Ventura, Calif.

Gina Ginsberg and C. H. Harrison
*How to Help Your Gifted Child:
A Handbook for Parents and
Teachers,* Monarch Press, New York, 1977

School superintendent Brandon Sparkman, writing with Ann Carmichael, offers parents the following tips to help a child learn:

Show a positive attitude toward school and learning.
Do not criticize your child's teacher to him.
Be secure enough to let your child be herself rather than
    your reflection.
Make constructive suggestions/criticisms to school officials.
Become involved in the school.[23]

That advice sounds terrific—and I have some more:

Ten Commandments for Rearing a Gifted Child

1. *Love.* Love is an emotional commitment to and involvement with your child. And, of course, it can be expressed in hundreds of attentive ways.

I like physical touching, so I was lucky that our GC also likes to cuddle. But researchers Schaffer and Emerson learned that not all infants respond well to "cuddliness," preferring instead to keep visual contact with their mothers when fearful or threatened.[24] I know that even though social and peer pressures will eventually change the degree of physical contact I share with my GC (I've already received a scornful "Mom!" when trying to kiss him good-bye at school), there are lots of other options available to me. (At 33, I know I can still look forward to a back rub from my mother.) Whatever method best

suits you and your GC, from a handshake to a hug, the point is
to demonstrate your affection. Don't expect your GC to be so
smart as to know it instinctively. And as my mother used to
say, "If your parents can't love you, who can?"

2. *Listen.* Look when you listen. If she knows you're listening, your GC will say something worth hearing.

One of my students at the university was a fortyish scholas-
tic newcomer. She told us she was taking the class for personal
growth and enrichment. For the rest of the semester, most of us
wanted to wring her neck. That woman talked continuously.
She could elaborate the most insignificant trivia. She had an
anecdote for every point in the lesson plan. She verbalized her
advice to anyone asking a question. Her daughter had done it
or her nephew had seen it or her husband had told her "this
was the way it was" when he went to college. It became one of
those dreadful teaching situations in which the entire class can
turn on one member besides coming to resent the teacher for
losing control. So I spoke to her about our predicament. She
was absolutely astounded.

"You know," she said, "I didn't realize I was talking so
much. I guess I'm not used to anyone really listening."

It is possible that she had spent twenty years talking end-
lessly to people who never listened or acknowledged. I see the
same thing happening to children who ramble and chatter
away to adults who are reading, relaxing or just simply being
"adult."

We also need to listen to more than words. I hate the trite
phrases of the nouveau-enlightened, but it is true that you
should "hear where your kid is coming from."

A simple example: For almost five years I bought our GC
what I thought was a wise, nutritious snack, something to show
my genuine worth as a mother—frozen carob-coated yogurt
bars. No Sugar Glumps or Chocolate Yummos for my kid: frozen carob-coated yogurt bars. But after a while, he stopped
asking for them. And after another while, he stopped eating
them. One day as I routinely plopped them into the grocery
cart, I heard a voice of dissent:

"I hate those stupid things."

"What?" was my incredulous reply.

"Every time you get those, I have to eat through that dumb chocolate stuff just to get to the good yogurt!"

Since I can't eat naked yogurt, I had assumed that was the way the kid liked it. He's now up to about a pack and a half per week of plain frozen yogurt bars. (Yuck!)

3. *Value learning.* My mother's family (like many others) had some very hard times in the depression of the 1930s. Grandfather lost his business. Grandmother had to sell the mementoes of her grandmother and eventually her own engagement ring. And every Christmas, after the gift orgy, we would hear the same old stories about the Christmas of 1931 when all Mother and each of her six sisters got was an orange and a new toothbrush.

"But your education is something no one can ever take away," she would say. "No matter how bad things are, what you have learned is always yours." I can still remember the somber chill of her voice.

My parents followed that philosophy to the letter. Mother spent hours going over my math homework and quizzing me on my Latin vocabulary. And it was a solemn occasion every six weeks as my father reviewed the report cards. I can't remember a time when I didn't simply assume that I had to be busy at learning.

You don't have to demand that your GC become a National Merit finalist or a Rhodes Scholar. You can show you value learning by one obvious method: read aloud. Read everything to a young GC: road signs, cereal boxes and the instructions on the towel dispenser in a public bathroom. Even a sophisticated GC of ten or eleven loves to be read to; especially if you read something considered grown-up like Michener, or Moynihan or the *Atlantic Monthly* (or *Sports Illustrated,* if that's all you've got). Reading is an extravagant, personal gift, perfect for any child.

4. *Talk.* Say something important about child things and about adult things. Talking to a child about child-oriented things does not mean talking to a child as if he had the mentality of a lamp. Baby talk is the classic example of talking to a

lamp. I'll go even further: baby talk is an abomination upon civilization, an affront to the human spirit, a rancorous, cruel and unnecessary handicap. If that weren't enough, it also does not make any sense. Why teach a child an unusable primary language? Why teach a child to say "ding-dong" when he has to learn later to say "penis"? Why teach a child "doggie" or "birdie" when she later must learn "beagle, a type of dog" or "buzzard, a type of bird"? Why would anybody do it? Is it because children are incapable of understanding real words? Is it just to be cute? (You know what I think of cute.) It has always seemed to me to be a rotten trick to pull on anybody, especially a kid.

From the very beginning, we spoke to our GC as if we expected him to remember and repeat what we said. When he asked, "What's that?" we used its real, standard, English name. If we didn't know, we found out and told him the next time.

Speech is, of course, a learned skill and much research verifies the notion that the way you communicate to your child makes quite a difference. One study comparing American and Japanese families showed that in both societies, the communication accuracy in mother/four-year-old child pairs accurately predicted the child's intellectual development one to two years later.[25]

The talk of a parent to a child becomes more than general background noise. The mere fact that it is directed to the child and challenges him to respond makes it a personalized and thus more effective linguistic stimulation.[26] Too many things in our society teach a child just to listen; you should also teach her to speak.

Sometimes you should talk about adult things. Talk about what worries you, what interests you, what surprises you, what makes you happy. Children, and especially bright, inquisitive GCs, need models for adult thought just as they need models for adult behavior.

5. *Spend time not money.* Burton White, through the Harvard study of infant development, concluded that during the second year of life (as the child becomes more physically active), the way in which parents respond becomes markedly in-

dividual. Leaving an almost universal set of baby responses, parents react in ways that were defined as (1) authoritarian, (2) permissive, or (3) compromising. (Yes, you have heard that before—it's based upon the original Sears studies.)

White theorized that the effective parent begins speaking to a child on a more sophisticated language level and provides activities and stimuli that advance with the child's development. Meanwhile, the ineffective parent will concentrate on (1) protecting the toddler from real or imagined injury, or (2) keeping her out of the way.[27] ("Kay, honey, this is an adult conversation.")

While adults certainly need time to be with *their* emotional and developmental peers (I mean, there must be verified cases of child-induced insanity), the more time you spend with your GC, the better he is for it.

Every parent picks individual battle lines. We have made a concerted effort to maintain two habits:

We eat meals with our GC. This is not as simple or as universal as it may sound to some of you. It's very easy to hand the kid a hot dog and some raisins before the civilized adult dinner hour. Particularly in busy families, parents always have places to go, people to meet, things to do. If nothing else, a meal together forces you to sit down and look at one another. You may be arguing over whether or not he will actually choke on the broccoli, but at least it's communication.

We take our GC absolutely everywhere possible. This includes the theater, movies, a zoning board meeting, concerts, antique auctions, my haircut appointment, a tennis tournament, museums, the car repair shop, the wallpaper store, the cat's examination at the vet's. Every place is a learning place. When things get rough, or fidgety—and they do—we leave. We do have adults' nights out, but almost every day activity includes the kid. Once when his school was on holiday, I took our GC to a faculty meeting at the university. He sat enthralled as my colleagues brilliantly debated the profound ramifications of a coin-operated coffee maker.

I remember discussing this point with the mother of another GC. We met in the library and I asked about her son (then almost seven).

"Oh, I'd never dream of bringing him in here," she answered. "He's so wild, he'd demolish the place. I drop him off at the sitter's and pick out some books he'd like."

"How will he ever learn not to demolish the place if he never comes?" I asked.

She said she'd never thought of it.

6. *Provide constructive materials.* And I do not mean worthless, commercial c---. Constructive materials would include paste, paper and scissors; old magazines; empty oatmeal boxes; blocks (I could light a candle for the Swede who invented Legos); a deck of cards; a ball; discovery equipment and toys that require a child to do something.

Every item you add to your child's environment is an essential one because a child begins to learn at hour one, day one. And the consumption of the environment is incredibly intense. As the parent of a GC, your first challenge may be the recognition of your child's unique and/or accelerated abilities. It seemed as if we were always the last to know any given level Stuart had reached. He was constantly surprising us with what he could do. We had particular difficulty knowing what level toys to select. (I'll give you one clue: don't believe the ages recommended by the toy manufacturers.)

Most frustrating were the "ill-chosen" birthday and Christmas gifts. I remember the wooden Fisher-Price puzzles. They seemed like a fantastic idea: educational, brightly painted, perfect for all sorts of mental and manual exercises. I told everyone who asked for a gift idea, "Stuart would love a Fisher-Price wooden puzzle." He got six puzzles that Christmas—two labeled "for ages 2-4" and four labeled "for ages 3-6." He ripped off the plastic wrap, dumped the pieces for all six in a pile and began reassembly. Within the time it takes to clean up the wrapping paper and pour another eggnog, he had successfully put them together. He was 2½. He never showed the slightest interest in any of the puzzles from that day forward.

Most "storebought" toys would amuse him for only short periods of time. The simple but creatively inspiring variety had much more durability. He would spend an hour stacking blocks or empty oatmeals boxes. He would spend most of a day play-

ing with a ball or a cardboard plane. Measuring spoons, a magnet, magnifying glass, water and anything that floated, a flashlight, anything on a string, anything that rolled or bounced—
these were his favorite playthings from infancy until about age
four and the fantasy period.

Perhaps the smartest commercial-toy decision I ever made
was the week I put half of the grocery money on a Lego Universal Building Set. Legos, those tiny, bright plastic building components, have survived for years as our recreational mainstay.
Loving grandparents, aunts and uncles have since added to a
collection that could fill a good-sized bread box. Legos have become an integral part of our household, showing up as space
ships, rocket launchers, police cars, small buildings landscaping
the houseplants, participants in the silverware drawer, a surprise in the chair cushions for unwary guests and a primitive
alarm system for any barefooted burglar. My only complaint is
the way they clog the vacuum.

(We also went through the gun period. From the beginning,
I was dead-set against guns—no pun intended. The day he
ripped up two curves of model train track and stuck them in his
belt, I knew I had lost. So, I bought him a Star Wars gun instead of Easter candy. It haunted me for years as he continually made reference to "that Easter gun.")

The degree to which you want to construct an activity
schedule is, of course, a very personal decision. In her book,
Teach Your Baby, Genevieve Painter suggests daily lesson
plans for the intellectual stimulation of an infant. In conjunction with a day care center in Mt. Carmel, Illinois (sponsored
by the University of Illinois), Painter developed a research
project aimed at determining whether or not babies who were
"tutored" for one year would exhibit greater increases in IQ
scores than would the nontutored control group. And, of
course, they did.

The program included three types of activities for babies
eight to twenty-four months old:

Lone activities before sleep and after awakening (crib toys).
Activities for informal play.
Short structured daily lessons of uninterupted play. These

sessions were fifteen minutes long as soon as the baby could sit alone, and then advanced to one hour. The activities in the lessons (puzzles, stringing beads, pegs-in-holes, rolling the ball, etc.) became increasingly complex as the baby's skills developed.

All these structured activities took place in a special corner, with a special set of "learning" toys that the child came to associate with the lessons. (Pavlov would be proud.) After one year, the experimental group averaged 10 points higher on individual IQ tests. The following year, Painter taught mothers to teach the babies. One year later, this group averaged 16 points higher than did the control group.[28]

Similar research reported by the University of North Carolina[29] and Cornell professor Urie Bronfenbrenner[30] suggests that early intervention programs (head start, kindergarten, special learning projects for targeted disadvantaged children, etc.) are far more successful when parents (particularly the mother) are taught to teach the child.

In addition, I think it's important to require a maturing GC to develop her own interests and activities. So we have created our "project-periods." At close intervals (nothing rigidly scheduled), we select a time to work together, but on separate projects. Stuart is told that it's time for him to come up with his own project because his father and I are busy on our own. Naturally we hope this will help build his sense of self-direction and independence. At least it allows me to get something done for myself once in a while.

7. *Expect something.* In the "olden" days, most children did the chores. No plan, no analysis—things simply had to be done. Lots of modern-day GCs miss that. Routine household assignments are the easiest way to start. You have to be somewhat careful, because if you assign tasks that are overpowering, you merely build in a frustration factor and ensure failure. All these decisions are relative and individual. At three, our GC was absolutely overwhelmed with the problem of putting his playroom in order. At four, he could help when given specific directions: "Put all of the Legos in this box." And at five, he

started putting things away after they were used (except when he had friends over, when everything reverted to chaos). I'm not going to take much of the credit for this. His preschool teachers (both with many years experience with GCs) helped us to see that as cute and as cunning as he could be, he still was capable of putting away his toys. Believe me, there were days when I would chew on a stick rather than "do it myself."

At five our GC was responsible for the toy business; his personal hygiene; keeping dry food in the cat's dish; transporting his sometimes empty plate from the table to the sink; setting silverware and napkins for each meal; putting dirty clothes in the hamper; opening the plastic bags for yard cleanup; picking paper cups out of the bushes after his friends had snacks; retrieving any toys left in the yard at the end of the day. (Believe me, it was hard sending a little kid out into the night with a flashlight and a grocery bag, but I told myself it would surely build his character.) Unlike an extra half-hour of TV, these things were constant and nonnegotiable.

In the early days, discipline seemed only a physical response in our family: one quick swat to the rear end when Stuart (1) chewed on the houseplants, (2) chewed on the telephone cord, (3) headed for the street, or (4) did anything else likely to cause him more grievous physical harm than would the swat.

Those researchers at Harvard were so right, because as he became a toddler, life became more complicated. The swatting offenses multiplied. It seemed I was scolding and swatting or swatting and scolding all day. Stuart himself was the one who brought the matter to the floor for a vote. One day, after being scolded and swatted for a habitual crime (spitting on the cat), he turned and calmly said, "Mother, spanking is not a good idea because it just doesn't work anymore. I only stand there crying—it doesn't keep me from doing bad things. We have to think of something else."

I know psychiatrists who would throw up their notepads over who was in charge at that moment, but the kid had a point worth considering. His views were certainly substantiated by many experts. In an essay to teachers of the gifted, Dr. Joanne Whitmore concludes: ". . . it is wise to help them [GCs] identify and evaluate the consequences of specific behaviors, develop an understanding of their self-control problems and design alternative ways of handling emotions and needs to prevent the negative consequences produced by the 'undesirable social behavior.' "[31] Obviously, "I'm gonna bust your butt" (a charming phrase our GC picked up from a neighborhood friend) simply wasn't going to cut it anymore.

Whitmore suggests five strategies for alternative discipline, and I've tried four of the five.

Dialogue. "In the dialogue process, the gifted child will learn to identify and evaluate the social and personal consequences of the behavior in question." ("We're going to sit down and calmly discuss why you're driving your mother stark-raving mad." Right! Maybe hers did, but mine didn't.)

Help the gifted child develop a rational understanding of the problem behavior. ("I want you to sit on this chair until you can behave or until you can tell me why you're driving your mother stark-raving mad.")

3. *Class meetings* ". . . in which the teacher invites a child with a special problem at school to share it with classmates and seek their assistance." (I *hate* this one! Although it could be modified for in-home use, it reeks of a cute little sensitivity session with an amateur analyst at the helm! The potential for problem creation is overwhelming. If your kid ever comes home with news of this technique, I would strongly suggest that you check it out.)

Behavior modification techniques. Behavior modification, affectionately nicknamed "M & M Therapy" because therapists at first used M & M candies for rewards, consists of immediate reward, lack of reward, or punishment relative to desired behavior. It's the way trainers teach chickens to turn on light bulbs. Whitmore very accurately points out that, all too often, a GC can learn to outsmart the game.

Never underestimate your GC's ability. We wanted to provide some mathematical stimulation for Stuart, so we bought one of those video games. (Learning machines and programmed instruction are based upon simple forms of behavior modification.) The problem appeared on the screen. A correct answer earned the reward of a flashing smile and an electronic fanfare. An incorrect answer displayed an electronic stick figure who got the buzzer, hung his head (in implied shame) and marched off the screen. After an hour of blissful attentiveness, our GC learned that he could hit the reset button two times in quick succession, override the circuitry and cause the correct answer to flash on the screen with no human brain power required.

It wasn't a total waste. The package also included a word-scramble game where one person "types" a word, electronically scrambles the letters and challenges the second person to figure out the original. Stuart loves this puzzle and has become very good at visually unscrambling even multisyllabic phrases. (But we have to watch him, because he'll cheat by peeking while you're typing the problem.)

Involvement of the student in developing self-management skills. The GC is encouraged to set time limits for activities, select alternatives, make plans, decide responsibilities, punishments, etc.

Once when I was teaching a class of eighth-graders, I decided to try the then avant-garde method of self-managed discipline. The class developed a code of class behavior, a system of rewards and punishments and a judicial review process. They drew up a contract and everyone agreed to abide by democratic rule. I really felt pleased with them and myself. Then we tried to put the whole thing into practice. A relatively minor offense would turn into something akin to the McCarthy hearings and a more serious transgression would blossom into the Nuremberg Trials.

I'll accept full responsibility for the failure. I don't mean to discourage you from attempting self-management plans. (All of you business majors will no doubt recognize Management-By-Objectives.) In fact, self-discipline is a primary goal of all child-rearing practices. I'm simply warning you about building in enough checks and balances. Particularly when dealing with a young GC, appoint yourself a combination President/Supreme Court Chief Justice.

Aside from these methods, I've also tried intimidation,

emotional tirades and simple bribery. I don't know what works and what doesn't. I hope someday our GC will write a book and tell me. Most experts talk about plain old-fashioned discipline using terms like consistency and fairness which, like many concepts, are easier to talk about than to put into practice!

It's terribly hard being a consistent parent. I even have trouble with consistency in my own life decisions. But mastering this skill is a key to parental success and that alone makes it worth the effort.

Your mistakes in this regard are difficult to hide from a GC. For one thing, he can very often remember exactly what you said the last time a specific subject arose. When you're heavily into your parenting role, it's very difficult to control your temper (or laughter) as your previous dictums are repeated with phonographic fidelity. "No, what you said was that the next time I put the cat in the drawer, I'd have to go without dessert for a week." You can find yourself treating accuracy as a compound felony. No sense in accusing him of being disrespectful. He thinks he's only being precise.

And in a world of a million details, let he who has never forgotten which kid was told to clean up the bathroom cast the first stone. I've taken to making lists. "Today I told Stuart *a, b, c.* Follow up on *d, e, f.*"

Fairness: What's fair? Is it fair to tell a kid to be quiet because you don't want any noise? It certainly never seemed fair to me when I was a kid. Can you be fair when you see only the results, not the cause of the transgression? Can you fairly punish a kid for having a "smart aleck" look on her face? I was always being punished for "looking smart aleck" when I rarely had control over whatever my face was doing. Can you teach judgment only by punishing the lack of it?

My disciplinary technique has evolved into what I call "The Modified Positive Alternative Selection Method."

"Okay, Stuart, you have two choices. You can either put your X-wing fighter back in your room, where it belongs, or you can throw it in the trash. Take your pick."

I know it sounds like a threat, but he always decides to put it away.

I have learned a great disciplinary technique from one of our son's teachers. When I give him a correcting instruction, I hold his face in my hands and clearly, calmly state my position. It probably won't work when he's sixteen. But while he's young, he seems to take it all more seriously than when I scream and flail my arms.

8. *Encourage fantasy and creativity.* The drifting between fantasy and creativity seems to be less clearly defined than are most other concepts of child-rearing. Expert discussion of fantasy in children is usually from one of three vantage points: Freudian psychology, behavioral psychology and developmental psychology.

Freudians talk about fantasy in terms of preadolescence, latency and potentially painful Oedipal possibilities.* Some of the Freudian literature is so alarmist as to (as they say in Indiana) "scare the waddin' out of you."

If you don't do this, your kid will grow up to be like this. If you do that, your kid will be one of those. Over the years, I have come to see the Freudians as a religious cult—you either believe them or you don't. I don't.

Behavioralists will tell you that fantasy with purpose is a useful, even admirable quality. Creativity is the best kind of fantasy because it produces a usable resource. (One expert cited the invention of indoor plumbing as a bit of fantasizing that was of particular social value.) Consequently, when fantasy is merely a means to escape the task at hand, it becomes of no real value and must be corrected (by behavior modification, of course).

I personally found this attitude of the useful fantasy and the useless fantasy hard to take. It requires parents to make some pretty shaky decisions: "Okay, Peter, pretending to be a dog is out, unless you can come up with a new slant on hydrant design. Kate, darling, it's perfectly acceptable for you to make believe you're a mommy—it'll be good practice."

---

* For a clear, open-minded interpretation of the Oedipus theories and myths, I would suggest you read *Understanding Children* by Richard A. Gardner, M.D. (Jason Aronson, New York, 1973). Dr. Gardner is a professor of child psychiatry at Columbia University and has a great many interesting things to say about the entire subject of child rearing.

Developmentalists see the fantasy period as one step in the healthy matriculation called growth. When looking through developmental literature, you will find fantasy described in nonthreatening terms, such as role playing and make-believe.

Burton White observed that the role play of three- to six-year-olds took on distinct patterns. He believed that those who were developing normally primarily fantasized in adult roles, such as doctors, truck drivers and fictional super-heros. Children not developing according to norms for the age selected roles that involved regression (babies) or more modest aspirations (such as animals or tree stumps). He concluded, "Some parents may feel that somehow or other the child's grasp on reality will be loosened if he is encouraged in unreal kinds of talk and play. Our observations suggest otherwise."[32]

Sometimes you need to give in and be Princess Leia to your GC's (Luke, Han, Chewbacca). Many were the days I would be blocked from entering a room while a three-foot Luke Skywalker cleared my path of menacing Stormtroopers.

"Okay, Princess, you can come in now. I got 'em all with my lightsaber!"

(My feminist blood would rise a degree or two as I always reminded him that Leia was a feisty little lady, quite capable of blasting a few Stormtroopers on her own—that is, if she hadn't been carrying the laundry.)

Dr. Fredelle Maynard in *Guiding Your Child to a More Creative Life* makes the following suggestions for parents who wish to help a child discover and develop creativity:

- Teach your child to see and observe what's around him.
- Encourage your child to record discoveries, thoughts and questions on paper, tape or film.
- Create a home environment that is individual and varied.
- Display your child's creations as well as reproductions of "great art."
- Encourage your child's curiosity and sense of exploration.
- Avoid the sexist stereotypes associating art with effeminacy.
- Encourage independence and decision making.
- Don't demand perfection.

- Let your child progress at her own pace.
- Respect your child's rights.
- Establish values and standards.[33]

The message is clear:

Give your GC blank paper and crayons, not coloring books.
Let him sleep crosswise in bed if he wants to.
Don't turn up your nose if he likes catsup on his eggs.

9. *Pump the ego.* To hell with what they say about other people's kids, the best gift you can give any child is a strong self-image.

It's time to discuss the "locus of control" theory. If a child is taught that most environmental factors are in his control, he tends to develop an internal locus of control: "I'm in charge of my life. I can make a difference." If a child is taught that environmental factors are beyond his control, he tends to develop external control: "They probably won't let me do that. I'd better wait to see what happens."

If we believe that, as a group, GCs possess the greatest potential for human intellectual development, reasoning and the analysis of problems, leadership and creativity, we don't want these people running around unsure of "who's in charge." We want them to be in charge, at least of themselves. Why would we want this vast potential for universal human development sitting around waiting for someone else to read the stars or the cards or the bones?

This is what happens when the parents of a GC omit or overlook or bungle the job of developing the child's ego strength. It has been aptly said by Juliana Gensley, Professor Emeritus, California State University, "An adult who sincerely believes he must do all the thinking because a child cannot cope, will produce a child who cannot cope, who has no faith in himself, or in the universe."[34]

Don't worry about turning your GC into an egomaniac. There are more than enough (elements, people, events) out there capable of "knocking her down to size."

Some techniques for elementary ego pumping:

- When your child dresses for school, combs his hair or steps out of his bath, tell him he looks fantastic, or sharp, or whatever word suits you.
- Ask her what she thinks about something important.
- Ask her what she thinks about something trivial.
- Tell him when he's done a good job at something.
- Let her hear you tell someone else how proud you are of her.
- When you're in public places, look at him, smile at him and generally acknowledge your special relationship.
- Thank her when she does something worthy of gratitude.
- Respect his privacy.
- Say "please" when you're asking for a favor.
- Always be ready to come to her defense. Where is it written that you must always be judiciously impartial when it comes to your own kids?

And for the final commandment of GC rearing:

10. *Turn off the TV sometimes.* It was hard for me to say that, because I personally love TV. I love to listen to Cavett and Buckley and MacNeil/Lehrer. I will change my life-style so that I can stay awake for Monty Python. I love watching Nick and Nora Charles in the 1934 version of *The Thin Man* and Jonathan and Jennifer Hart in the 1980 remake. The point I try to keep in mind is that we didn't have a TV in my childhood home until I was almost thirteen. And that's a bit different from my son's tube-fed generation of "Sesame Street" veterans.

If you ever find yourself with a week with nothing to do— try reviewing the expert testimony on the sins and virtues of television. The educational impact of television cannot be overstated. Television teaches our kids and that's all there is to that. The only debate is centered upon what it teaches, how it teaches and to what final extent. Even those purists among you who smugly proclaim that your kids watch "only one hour each day," or that you've forever banished the tube from your home, cannot escape its reach. Television has so pervaded our culture that its influence will still reach you and yours. Even the most basic elements of your life are affected by TV. Many of the

products available to you are, by and large, available because a
TV audience survey showed that people needed and/or wanted
them. Items such as electric hot dog cookers, breath mints,
Mork suspenders and Veg-a-matics might never have been developed without the influence of the tube. You can now buy
bread with no preservatives, be taken off junk mailing lists,
drive safer cars and expound the virtues of vitamin C because
of conversations that took place on television talk shows. Your
children, if barred from TV, will become culturally handicapped. (Oh, yes they will!) Watch a group of ten-year-olds who
discover that one of their number has never heard of Arnold,
Buck or 240 Robert. Your kids are going to be above all that?
Not in this lifetime. Television will not go away. You may as
well wish for the return of the nickel candy bar.

If you believe the results of one 1976 study, your child probably will choose to watch those TV shows that are similar to
your family's communication pattern.[35] The implication is that
if your family is verbal and highly analytical, your kids will
watch programs such as "Face the Nation," "Washington
Week in Review," and "Bill Moyers' Journal." If your family
communicates in monosyllabic grunts, your kids may choose
lighter, less demanding fare, such as "Sheriff Lobo," "Real
People," and "Bullwinkle." (Obviously any conclusion of this
kind drifts into the realm of interpretation.)

One enterprising Ph.D. candidate studied "The Role of
Televised Sports in the Socialization of Political Values of Adolescents." Testing the premise that levels of conservative political values were related to the viewing of televised sports, he in-
terviewed over 600 students. His conclusions were that TV
sports may be reinforcing such "conservative" political values
as "system support, loyalty and the discouragement of dissent."[36]

Researchers at the University of Pennsylvania revealed significant discrepancies in a child's TV viewing habits as reported
by the parents and as reported by the child himself. Parents
consistently proclaimed:

Shorter viewing times
Stricter household rules about content

More co-viewing and parent/child interaction

Lower susceptibility to commercials ("My kid knows that Sugar Rotters and Gut Strippers are less nutritious than are their boxes and labels.")

Not only that—all you out there in "parent-never-never-land"—parental exaggeration increased with social/economic class.[37] Higher-ups in the socioeconomic ladder either (1) have greater fear of the effects of TV, (2) have less real knowledge of their children's habits or (3) lie more. Take your pick.

Sides in the debate have been clearly drawn. Attitudes toward TV range all the way from "It's criminal" to "It's actually quite fantastic."

IT'S CRIMINAL

According to many, TV is criminal because:

It is used as a babysitter. (This argument is always proposed by someone who has never tried simultaneously to dress for a party, keep the bathroom clean, preserve the integrity of the cheese ball tray and not beat the kids.)

It makes children passive watchers, not doers.

TV causes entertainment expectations that cannot be met by teachers and other real-life situations. (My sister, a first-grade teacher, once complained that she couldn't always dress up in her Big Bird suit, just to teach the alphabet.)

It encourages Pavlovian regulation rather than real discovery. (This charge was often made about the rapid-fire pace of educational programs such as "Sesame Street" and "The Electric Company.")

It gives information that is vast but out of context and confusing. If you had to guess which stimulus is more influential on students, TV or an adult who is responding to their questions and confusions, which would you choose? Countless research studies again and again verify what seems like common sense: children benefit more from adult stimulus and response than they benefit from TV (even "Mr. Rogers").[38]

I will admit that I'm set back a bit when I have to explain

some of the disjointed things our GC hears on TV. For example: "You could be wearing the wrong bra."

Television reinforces misinformation and a bad example of the language. (Personally I cringe at the nice little blonde in the tampon commercial who smiles and tells us "It's been proved...." And one of the highly rated educational programs—"Zoom"—continually exhibits youngsters who zoomed out of English class with subject/verb inconsistencies and sloppy diction.)

But it was a commission headed by Milton Eisenhower that leveled the most severe condemnation—that children, particularly young children, often cannot discriminate between fact and fantasy.[39] If it's on TV, it must be true.

Social scientists and others have repeatedly observed educational declines in college-level students. Mostafa Rejai, professor of political science, Miami University, lays the blame right in front of the TV set.

"In a word, the child grows up believing that the world comes in a series of effort-free, seven-minute segments. No wonder Johnny cannot read. No wonder he cannot write. No wonder he is totally incapable of concentration."[40]

In a study of 250 gifted elementary students, Dr. Stanley Stern tested levels of creativity before and after three weeks of concentrated television viewing. Seven groups of students watched one of six program categories: educational TV, cartoons, sports, comedies, drama and a combination of all five. The control group was given no specific instructions.

The members of the control group showed an increase in creativity (pre- and posttests of the Guilford Test of Creativity) while in five of the groups there was a notable decrease in every area except verbal abilities. The greatest decrease was in the area of figure production. Also apparent was a decrease in the students' abilities for flexible thinking. Those GCs who watched only cartoons experienced the greatest decreases in creativity scores. Most surprising was the fact that the group watching drama (including violence) slightly increased creative performance.[41]

Of course, there's more. Drabman and Thomas set up an

experiment in which third-graders were shown either a violent TV show or a baseball game. They then witnessed a real-life fight between two younger children. (I can't help but be curious as to how they staged that one.) It was concluded that the exposure to TV violence decreased the children's readiness to summon adult help and/or intervene.[42]

George Gerbner, in an article entitled "About the Anxiousness of Heavy Viewers," presented results suggesting a relationship between frequent TV viewing and high levels of anxiety about the amount of violent crime in real life.[43] This negative aspect of all media was expressed in "Sowing the Seeds of Anxiety" by Juliana Gensley: "A gifted child who sees the world through TV, radio or the front page can easily despair of the fate of the world."[44]

And to give you a moment's pause: As reported in the *Scandinavian Journal of Psychology,* preschoolers were videotaped and studied while they were watching TV violence—physical, cartoon and verbal—as well as nonviolence. The children's facial expressions and reactions were judged by an impartial panel of child therapists and educators. Of the four categories, physical violence evoked more expression of fear and worry, while the children exhibited characteristics of anxious "withdrawal" from scenes of verbal violence between adults.[45]

Finally, in the "I always knew it!" or "You must be kidding!" category: A study comparing the TV viewing habits of fifty adolescents "extensively involved" with marijuana and two control groups reported that the "heavy users" were also "heavy viewers."[46]

While scientific research and empirical study can be interpreted in numerous ways, the "antitelevisionists" do have some very strong arguments.

There's that insidious matter of marketing our children to TV sponsors. We all know by now that the real product of commercial TV is the audience. The attention of our children is sold by TV stations and networks to the toy makers, cereal makers and assorted entrepreneurs. These people are pros. They spend a lot of bucks and computer tape figuring out just whose kids will buy just what gadget. To mention only one example published in the *Journal of Advertising Research,* advertisers were told that extensive analysis of "Parental Responses to Child Marketing" revealed that parents were most influenced toward a purchase by the child who said he saw it on TV, and by premium offers that appealed to children. (I'll admit it. I confess! I made a special trip to Burger King because our GC saw on the tube that they were offering "The Empire Strikes Back" glasses with every soft drink.) A sad and most revealing third conclusion was that health appeals had little or no effect on what parents bought for their children.[47]

In a discussion of TV marketing, educator Gladys Jenkins says that parents are forever faced with mounting pressures to buy what the kids see on TV. And turning off the set is too simplistic because your kids are also trying to keep up with the Joneses' kids. She speaks of accepting the reality and developing some positive means of dealing with it. Define your child's needs, wants and wishes.[48]

Needs, of course, are essentials such as nourishing food, clothing and even fluoride toothpaste. Needs can also be a few of those things that satisfy a child's need to belong to a peer group. ("But Mom, all the kids have a Millennium Falcon.")

Wants are stimulated by everything on TV and are very often only temporary. Jenkins reminds parents that too many "I wants" can be the sign of a child with a low self-image ("Gotta have those goodies to prove I'm somebody") or boredom ("Nothing else to do—why not get a goodie?")

Wishful thinking is composed of those wants the child knows are not likely to come true. ("I wish I could have my very own tiger.")

Parents must strike a balance between being a teacher of consumerism and being a scrooge. Everybody deserves something a little crass or tacky sometimes; and occasionally, a child should be able to have something extravagant simply because it's good for the soul. Materialism is not going away, Jenkins stresses; so teach your child how to judge what is worth buying. (I think that's why somebody once invented allowances.)

Also included in the indictment against TV commercials is the child's sense of frustration and envy when he cannot get all the goodies seen on the screen. I know that I'm the parent. I know that I do not have to (and I don't) always buy it, but it does turn the shaft a bit when I realize that my kid has a deep-rooted belief that something's lacking in a day without Bubblicious.

TV and its ensuing sophistication exposes children to some realities that may be a bit premature, even for a GC. Talk of rape, incest, murder, a live-insta-cam-news-view of a police shootout—they all seem to spring up without warning. It can of course be said that all knowledge dispels innocence; and no matter how painful, that's the way it is. We can't go back. I'm expressing a frustration here rather than a real indictment. It's hard finding an answer for the five-year-old GC who asks why the girl on TV had an abortion, and what is it anyway?

For me, the biggest flaw of TV is the way it reinforces the negative and the incorrect. A prime example is the game show.

At first, I thought the purpose of TV game shows was to provide display pictures for the people who sell TV sets. Now I see the phenomenon as something more sinister. TV game shows teach our children that the best things in life are merchandise, and they can be free if you pick the right curtain; sexual stereotypes are alive and living in California; greed and stupidity get the audience reaction. Every day, Joe Doe and Annie Advertising Assistant—people just like Mom and Dad—win something for nothing. Must they struggle for years in academia? Must they work an honest day's labor? Must they overcome personal trauma through courage and stamina of will? Do we have any evidence that they even floss their teeth regularly? No. They simply must roll doubles on a pair of giant dice, pick the right box or recognize the phrase:

E v e — y B o o b y H a s I t s P — i z e .

Female contestants are most often introduced in terms of marital status, quantity and ages of children and hobbies. A professional woman often must work in "I'm also a pediatric neurosurgeon" after the first commercial. Males are most often introduced in terms of occupation, hobbies, life goals and, if there's time, family affiliation.

What's really frightening are the attitudes such giveaways

nurture: "Take a chance 'cause it's all one big crap throw anyway." "I already have two cars, but so what; I'm playing until I win that Thunderbird." "Why be satisfied with a measly $5,000 when $25,000 is just sixty seconds away." "By God, knowing the name of that song is worth $100,000."

Game after game watching boob after boob win cars, cash, copper skillets and a kiss from the female assistant—no wonder every kid in America feels cheated without a set of Big Wheels.

It's Not So Bad

Many empirical studies find no correlation between heavy TV watching and negative behavior.[49] In fact, some educators are convinced that by the age of ten or twelve, children become completely saturated and the effects of TV watching decline markedly.[50] Such are also the beliefs of parents who say, "(Jeffy, Ali, Floyd) always sits in the room with the TV and ignores it."

In the true fence-straddling it's-not-so-bad tradition, one study reported that for adolescents:

1. The perception of reality and violence are highest when they view TV with parents.

2. Social learning is highest when viewing with parents.

3. Viewing TV with peers is seen as entertainment.[51]

It's Pretty Good

Much research has shown that rather than doing harm, TV can be a constructive element in the lives of our children. Wilbur Schramm concluded that GCs in particular watch more and learn more from TV.[52]

And while educational TV programs (such as "Sesame Street") were intended for children considered educationally disadvantaged, many researchers report considerable learning gains for those children with "the most developed cognitive base."[53]

Particularly in the areas of vocabulary and data gathering, TV exposure to facts and events is undeniably a positive educational experience. I can think of a great many things our GC has learned from TV:

Cigarette smoking probably causes cancer.

Violence is present in our society, and it is evil. (TV helps a child learn this without requiring him to experience violence firsthand.)

Killer whales were misnamed because they're not killers after all.

People don't like being near you if you have dandruff, bad breath or B.O.

He also knows, because of TV, what it looks like on the surface of Venus, how to read weather radar and something about people and places in distant parts of the globe. (We would like to take him around the world, but TV lets him see the Russian Steppes, the Great Wall and the Arctic Circle while we save for the boat fare.)

IT'S ACTUALLY QUITE FANTASTIC

It is in the area of positive social skills and insight into human behavior that TV can really come off like a star. "Prosocial" is the word used to describe those TV programs specifically developed to illustrate personal problems and solutions, as well as events of human interaction. These would include programming such as the "After School Specials" and classical drama. Prosocial TV carries with it the stimulus for class discussion and related activities, as well as a plain old-fashioned conversation with your kid. The key, of course, is adult participation.

Researchers from Pennsylvania State University studied prosocial TV alone and with adult-led training (verbal labeling and role play) as it was seen by seventy-three kindergartners. They concluded that children do learn prosocial content (particularly when reinforced by follow-up training) *and* can generalize that learning to other situations.[54]

A study of a specific TV series, "Inside/Out," showed that it was a tremendous aid in helping eight-to-ten-year-olds deal with personal and social development. The program, developed by the Agency for Instructional Television, gave a very structured look at the anxiety-producing events in a preadolescent's life. Discussion questions and group activities accompanied the program.[55] Educational TV of this sort becomes an effective tool for both parent and classroom teacher.

What we shouldn't forget is that television, even the commercial variety, does have the potential for greatness. To its credit, the television industry has tried to establish some positives in the programs aimed at children. Attempts have been made to more clearly differentiate the tactics of the good guys from those of the bad guys. While reruns of "Starsky and Hutch" still make it difficult for a youngster to tell which killer is socially sanctioned and why, recent series such as "Chips" and "240 Robert" show helping adults reacting to violence in a more defensive and/or deterring fashion.

Let's be fair in this violence business; the TV industry didn't invent it all. Take a look at the first feature motion picture ever made in this country (Thomas Edison's *The Great Train Robbery*). Amidst the funny clothes and flickering waddles, you will see robbery, assault, hostage taking, a mail guard being blasted at close range, a passenger being shot in the back and a stoker being pounded into unconsciousness and flung off the moving train.

TV programming can dispel racial and sexual stereotypes if the producers will just set their corporate minds to it. This point was reinforced for me by our GC. One of his very favorite programs is the rescuing adventures of the sheriff's deputies of "240 Robert." In the program, the female lead happens to be a helicopter pilot. We once met a man who piloted the news helicopter for a local TV station. After the meeting, our (then four-year-old) GC said to me, "He probably wasn't a real helicopter pilot; he wasn't even a woman."

Much fabulously instructive programming does exist. I could rattle off titles like "Zoom," "Big Blue Marble," "Once Upon a Classic," "Disney's World," "Jacques Cousteau Specials," "Nova," etc. Enter exhibit A: "Mr. Rogers' Neighborhood."

The first time I saw Mr. Rogers, I thought to myself, "This guy is really a twink. He is not working on full wattage." I was definitely not an immediate fan. But as I began to listen to what he was saying and, more importantly, watch how our GC reacted to him, I changed my mind. We all have our own standards and philosophies of child rearing, and Mr. Rogers was saying everything that I believed and wanted a child of mine to hear. I like ideas like: "My body's fancy and so is yours"; "It's such a happy feeling to know you're alive"; "Scary-mad wishes can't really come true"; "I like to be told if it's going to hurt"; and "Let's make the most of this beautiful day."

I remember one emotional hurdle Mr. Rogers helped us over. During his fifth year, our GC went through the growing-independence, ego-building stage of hating Mom and Dad. This development was manifested by fits of anger, hostile plotting and sulking in his room. Then we watched an episode of Mr. Rogers. The lovely ingenue lead got so angry at two other characters that she went to a witch and learned how to turn them into snowmen; there followed the deed, repentance, ensuing resolution and time to kiss and make up. Finally, the concluding song stated the reassuring moral "Even good people do bad things sometimes." Every observant parent or teacher has seen it—that beautiful human facial expression that accompanies the dawn of an idea. "Oh, yeah," his face said, seeming to understand suddenly that he was really okay, still on safe ground. He certainly could have learned the same lesson by reading Mark Twain, or Dostoevski, but Mr. Rogers was there at just the right time. When, at some time in the future, every household has a videotape recorder as well as a TV, tapes of Mr. Rogers will be library classics and family heirlooms.

If we believe TV has "ruined" our children, we have not been deceived or deluded or denigrated without fully cooperating. Any betrayal is self-induced because a TV set never pretended to be a surrogate parent, an electronic social vanguard or even a decent pet. TV is just what it has always been: a fun machine. An item to be used or not used by judicious choice, it's no different from a bike or a pachinko table. Did you ever consider turning your kid over to the care of a player piano? The point is hardly original, but it merits repeating. Watch what your child is watching and *decide* whether it is what you want her to be shown and told. You may sanction the sociological overtones of "Starsky and Hutch." You may think the soaps are healthy outlets for normal animal passions. You may even think that "Diff'rent Strokes" is a credible premise. What counts is the conscious selection.

In *The World of the Gifted Child,* Priscilla Vail suggests how parents of GCs can use TV constructively:

> Have the child read the weekly TV schedule and circle choices. Go over the choices and ask your GC for reasons why one show may be suitable and one may not.
>
> Ask the GC to record predictions of what a show will be about.
>
> After the program (particularly if you cannot watch) ask your GC for a review of what he has seen and any comments about what he learned.[56]

This technique could easily be adapted by those parents with specific viewing allocations as the GC could participate in the selection of available hours and make active decisions as to whether or not the choice was worth it.

I'll just repeat: turn off the TV sometimes, and your kid will survive. Now it's time for commandment number 11.

11. *Lighten up.* Learn to be a resource, not a tour guide through your GC's life. Rearing a kid is like teaching someone to ice skate: your success is measured by how little they need you to hold them up.

Imagine your very best adult friend. You like most of what she does and says. You respect her right to differ; after all, you don't have everything in common. You want happiness and all good things for her, but there are limits to how much you can influence her life. It's a two-way street; you both bring things of value to the relationship. You share a common history because you've grown and matured together. You know that after you have your (fun, intellectually stimulating, loving) times, you go home to your own privacy and she goes home to hers.

I think that rearing a child should be thought of as training a person to become one of your adult friends—certainly one of your most precious friends, but a self-reliant, independently functioning friend, nonetheless—*never* a grown-up child or a possession. Your dog you can possess. Your African violets you can possess. Your kid has to be transplantable some day.

What Turns Mother Gray

Occasionally I will run across someone who sees it as his or her sacred duty to tell me again how we must strive to make our GCs "normal." For a long time these diatribes infuriated me. Then I realized they were talking "normal" on one plane and I was assimilating "normal" at another.

For most people, a normal child is one who is well integrated into his chronological peer group, kind to animals and polite to adults. A normal child won't spit in your face or break the fingers of his cousins. When they were telling me our GC should be normal, they meant he should be socially appropriate. I don't believe this kind of normalcy has very much to do with intellectual or creative potential. I have known several cases where the parents of severely retarded or profoundly handicapped children (for whatever reasons, guilts or rationalizations) allowed their kid's behavior to slip well below socially appropriate standards and well below the child's capabilities. There is a common misconception that a bright, gifted individual is usually an insufferable brat. Part of me wonders if it isn't sometimes a convenient rationalization. "Well, yes, she is gifted, but she's so obnoxious with it." At any rate, most everyone seems pleasantly surprised when a genius is also a nice guy.

I will admit there is a fine line between positive and negative qualities here.

> How do you teach a child to value his abilities and yet not be vain?
>
> How do you teach a child to be unpretentious and yet proud?
>
> How do you teach a child to be assertive and yet not overpowering?
>
> How do you teach a child to be considerate and yet not patronizing?

It's not as easy as picking out a noble goal and saying, "I'm going to teach my kid to be good."

We all want our kids to grow to be decent adults. While the definition of "decent" may vary, I doubt that many people set out to rear a societal degenerate or a homicidal maniac.

When someone runs amok, it seems to be the parents who throw up their hands and say, "I don't understand it. She was such a good little girl!" or "Whose kid is that, anyway?"

I'm not trying to hype the idea that day-to-day, bunker-to-bunker parenting is easy. No one has ever mistaken me for Pollyanna. But one way of allowing your child to ripen to so-cial/emotional growth and well-being is common sociological knowledge. No matter what changes or goes wrong, your child must grow up with four constant factors. Every child must:

1. Feel a part of a family unit. (Any variation or creative combination will do so long as it is loving.)
2. Feel responsibility to that family. (This involves more than "What will the neighbors think?")
3. Participate in the governing of that family. My parents (God love 'em) let each of us kids have one day a year (birthday, of course) to "govern" the family. We were in charge of everything, from what we ate for dinner to who got to sit in Daddy's chair. What lends a moral to this story is that none of us ever bent the privilege with anything truly outrageous (that is, if you don't count the year my sister had us eat spaghetti and french fries for three meals).
4. Know that rewards and punishments will be constant, appropriate and swift. (The Supreme Court should do so well!)

The Other Kids

Somehow you must get the message across. Your GC cannot deny himself, but neither can he wear combat boots through the intellectual guts of normal children. I personally think it's chauvinistic to teach your GC to value the feelings of others with an attitude that says: "We never kick cripples at our house," or "I always smile at dolts."

At the opposite pole from condescension, you can't accomplish anything by denying your child's giftedness and pretending she's like normal children. The other kids will notice the difference.

I remember Sarah. Sarah was eight and particularly intrigued with a four-year-old who could read.

"Did you just read that?" I once overheard her ask Stuart.

"Are you able to read?" she asked again, this time in total disbelief.

"Sure," was our GC's reply in his "can't everybody" attitude.

"I understand that Stuart can read," she said to me later. "How can he do that? I couldn't read until I was in the first grade and even then it was really hard."

The delicate balances of human interaction take most of us decades to perfect. And yet we often expect our children to do it instantly. Naturally, your goal is for your GC to be able to answer such questions for himself. You want him to discover how he will best relate to chronological peers and casual acquaintances. One noble goal may be a GC who sees her gifts as matters-of-fact. She has brown eyes, straight hair, high intelligence and an incredible talent with the language. Meanwhile, I think it's very hard to expect a young GC to know how to handle the curiosity of normal friends and associates. That leaves it up to you to be sensitive to the feelings of your GC's playmates.

I can't remember exactly what I told Sarah to ease what seemed to be a tiny bit of budding self-doubt—something about everybody being special in different ways and how she could probably do lots of things that Stuart hadn't learned yet. The best way of teaching your GC to be sensitive to others is to allow him to see you expressing some of that sensitivity yourself.

Life with Nongifted Siblings

It happens. It really does happen that one but not all of the children in a family will be a GC. When I see it happen, I'm glad I have an only child. Somehow you have to balance things: giving support and encouragement to your GC and not overpowering her normal siblings, letting all of your children grow to their capacities, being encouraging to one without being demanding to the other.

Above all, the common sense rule seems to be, avoid comparison. It can be hell to always hear about your little brother, the genius. And sometimes it's impossible to fill the footsteps of a gifted older sister. Encourage the uniqueness of each, but give to them in equal proportions. This includes equal time, equal attention and equal funds for education, hobbies and enrichment. If your GC—the one who's always winning the science fair—needs someone to drill her on organic chemistry formulas, do it. Then spend some time with the sibling who's still trying to learn the metric system.

Never expect different standards of behavior. I knew a family with three bright, normal children and one mathematical genius. He was endowed with a truly brilliant mind. He was also an outrageous little brat. Everytime Daniel pulled one of his "stunts" (like the time he decided to staple my living room drapes shut), his mother would defend him with, "We have to make allowances for Daniel, you know, he's different." This woman expected her other kids to follow the basic rules of civilized interaction, but Daniel was different. The only difference was the way she treated him.

When Failure Comes—And It Will

For some GCs, that first failure is an incredible shock. After years of whipping through homework and outguessing the teacher, a truly stimulating intellectual experience can bring on unexpected catastrophe. How we each work through failure is dependent upon many factors, but those methods most often selected by GCs are:

Blaming externals. "The teacher was stupid; the test was rotten; the other kids distracted me."

Internalizing guilt. "I'm really a sham. I never really was that smart after all. I can't fool people anymore."

Escapism. E. Paul Torrance has remarked that many GCs

never resolve the stress associated with eventual failures and so they simply stop trying. He concluded, "Some gifted students consistently fail because they never find anything they consider worth their best efforts."[57]

When you're a GC, working out your life is a very private tightrope. But contact with other GCs can make a difference. Every person benefits from the knowledge that he is somehow linked to other human beings, that his problems aren't really unique or weird or crazy. To know another GC who has also failed, to see another GC coping with a difficult situation, to have a chance to tell your story to a couple of understanding peers—these things mean more than a dozen lectures from your parents or a list of "To Do's" in any book on managing stress.

As the parent of a GC, your best strategies for helping your GC through failure are:

Keep your personal definitions of failure to yourself. Your GC defines her own failure, and nothing can be more compounding than something like: "Look, you'll get over it. Why, when I was your age ..."

Don't be a nag—be supportive.

Don't expect your GC always to be perfect. As Gina Ginsberg has observed, "That kind of halo makes for a very bad headache."[58]

One Final Note on Being a Successful Parent (See How I've Come to Accept My Role in This?)

We all like to think of people as individuals, separate models in and of themselves, a blending of all their experiences and self-initiated conclusions. But no matter how hard you squint at it, the fact is clear: any kid you rear is an awful lot like you.

I remember Jerry Juniper (definitely not his real name). Jerry was a good student, bright and inquisitive. He was also a royal pain in the gluteus maximus. He would hang around the teachers telling stupid jokes and guffawing all over them. He would always bring out the irrelevant in any class discussion. He was the first to catch a teacher's mispronunciation, error or omission. Physically he was what they call "gawky and gangly." He would slap you on the back, spill your coffee or have food on his face after lunch. It was unanimous. The teachers hated him. I was the counselor; so naturally they thought I could "cure" him.

After several conferences with Jerry, I honestly couldn't find anything seriously wrong. He loved school; he loved his home; he was perfectly happy with himself as well. He had some tentative career plans and an enthusiasm one would expect from any high schooler. He seemed so secure in his relationship with his family that I doubted the usual teacher's lounge diagnosis, "He just wants some attention."

Then I saw Jerry and his father at a basketball game. There they stood: father's arm around son's shoulder, totally engrossed in the spectacle, poking each other's ribs, having a perfectly marvelous time. Later, Jerry proudly introduced me to his dad. Mr. Juniper told a stupid joke and gave me an emphatic little punch to the upper arm while they guffawed in unison. He had popcorn hulls on his chin. I came to conclude that Jerry's school behavior was totally and undeniably correct. He was responding as he had been taught. He was following his role model. He was acting just like his dad. Before you probe too deeply into your child's behavior motivations, remember, in some way or another, he really only does what he sees you do.

Notes

1. Robert S. Albert, "Family Positions and the Attainment of Eminence: A Study of Special Family Positions and Special Family Experiences," *Gifted Child Quarterly*, 24:2, Spring 1980.

2. Ibid.
3. Walter B. Barbe, "A Study of the Family Background of the Gifted," *Journal of Educational Psychology,* 47:5, May 1956.
4. Charles J. Pulvino and Paul E. Lupton, "Superior Students: Family Size, Birth Order and Intellectual Ability," *Gifted Child Quarterly,* 22:2, Summer 1978.
5. Helen S. Astin, "Sex Differences in Mathematical and Scientific Precocity," *Journal of Special Education,* 9:1, Spring 1975.
6. Norma J. Groth, "Differences in Parental Environment Needed for Degree Achievement for Gifted Men and Women," *Gifted Child Quarterly,* 15:4, Winter 1971.
7. Lee Willerman and Miriam F. Fiedler, "Intellectually Precocious Preschool Children: Early Development and Later Intellectual Accomplishment," *Journal of Genetic Psychology,* 131:1, September 1977.
8. Robert R. Sears, "Sources of Life Satisfactions of the Terman Gifted Men," *American Psychologist,* 32:2, February 1977.
9. Deanna B. Radeloff, "Correlations of Creativity, Achievement and Parental Variables of Early School Entrance Children," *DAI,* 39:2A659, August 1978.
10. Robert R. Sears, E. E. Maccoby and H. Levin, *Patterns of Child Rearing,* Row, Pearson, Evanston, Ill., 1957.
11. Kevin J. Swick and Margo Willis, "Parents and Children in the Home Environment: Process and Product Implications for the School Setting," *Education,* 93:4, April–May 1973.
12. Craig R. Ramey, Dale C. Farran and Frances A. Campbell, "Predicting IQ from Mother-Infant Interactions," *Child Development,* 50:3, September 1979.
13. Norma J. Groth, "Mothers of the Gifted," *Gifted Child Quarterly,* 19:3, Fall 1975.
14. Peggy Stamp, "Girls and Mathematics: Parental Variables," *The British Journal of Educational Psychology,* vol. 49, part 1, February 1979.
15. Groth, "Mothers of the Gifted."
16. R. C. Nichols, "Parental Attitudes of Mothers of Intelligent Adolescents and Creativity in Their Mothers," *Child Development,* 35, 1964.
17. C. N. Banner, "Child Rearing Attitudes of Mothers of Under-Average- and Over-Achieving Children," *The British Journal of Educational Psychology,* vol. 29, part 2, June 1979.
18. Elizabeth Monroe Drews and John E. Teahan, "Parental Attitudes and Academic Achievement," *Journal of Clinical Psychology,* 13:4, October 1957.
19. Jack Divorin and Oakley Wyant, "Authoritarian Patterns in the Mothers of Schizophrenics," *Journal of Clinical Psychology,* 13:4, October 1957.

20. Rudolph Schaffer, *Mothering: The Developing Child Series.* Harvard University Press, Cambridge, Mass., 1977.
21. Henry Clay Lindgren, ed., *Reading in Educational Psychology,* Wiley, New York, 1968.
22. Albert, op. cit.
23. Brandon Sparkman and Ann Carmichael, *Blueprint for a Brighter Child,* McGraw-Hill, New York, 1975.
24. H. R. Schaffer and P. E. Emerson, "Patterns of Response to Physical Contact in Human Development," *Journal of Child Psychology and Psychiatry,* vol. 5, 1964.
25. W. Patrick Dickson et al., "Mother and Child as a Predictor of Cognitive Development in the United States and Japan," *Child Development,* 50:1, March 1979.
26. Schaffer, *Mothering.*
27. Burton L. White, *The First Three Years of Life,* Prentice-Hall, Englewood Cliffs, N.J., 1975.
28. Genevieve Painter, *Teach Your Baby,* Simon and Schuster, New York, 1971.
29. Ramey et al., op. cit.
30. Urie Bronfenbrenner, "Is Early Intervention Effective?" *Teacher's College Record,* vol. 76, December 1974.
31. Joanne R. Whitmore, "Discipline and the Gifted Child," *Roeper Review II,* December 1979.
32. White, op. cit.
33. Fredelle Maynard, *Guiding Your Child to a More Creative Life,* Doubleday, New York, 1973.
34. Juliana T. Gensley, "Sowing the Seeds of Anxiety," *Gifted Child Quarterly,* 21:4, Winter 1977.
35. John D. Abel, "The Family and Child Television Viewing," *Journal of Marriage and the Family,* 38:2, May 1976.
36. Robert H. Prisuta, "The Role of Televised Sports in the Socialization of Political Values of Adolescents," *DAI,* 38:10A, April 1978.
37. John R. Rossiter and Thomas S. Robertson, "Children's Television Viewing: An Examination of Parent-Child Consensus," *Sociometry,* 38:3, September 1975.
38. Jerome L. Singer and Dorothy G. Singer, "Can TV Stimulate Imaginative Play?" *Journal of Communication,* 26:3, Summer 1976.
39. "Statement on Violence in Television Entertainment Programs," National Commission on the Causes and Prevention of Violence, Milton Eisenhower, Chairman, U.S. Government Printing Office, Washington, D.C., 1969.
40. Mostafa Rejai, "On the Failure of Parents in the Educational Process," *Educational Forum,* 43:4, 1979.
41. Stanley L. Stern, "Television and Creativity: The Effect of Viewing Certain Categories of Commercial Television Broadcasting on

the Divergent Thinking Abilities of Intellectually Gifted Elementary Students," *DAI,* 34:7A, January 1974.
42. Ronald S. Drabman and Margaret H. Thomas, "Exposure to Filmed Violence and Children's Tolerance of Real Life Aggression," *Personality & Social Psychology Bulletin,* 1:1, 1974.
43. George Gerbner, "About the Anxiousness of Heavy Viewers," *Fernsehen und Bildung,* 12:1–2, 1978.
44. Gensley, op. cit.
45. Kristi M. Lagerspetz et al., "Facial Expressions of Pre-School Children While Watching Television Violence," *Scandinavian Journal of Psychology,* 19:3, 1978.
46. Jerome F. Brodlie, "Drug Abuse and Television Viewing Patterns," *Psychology,* 9:2, May 1972.
47. Pat L. Burr and Richard M. Burr, "Parental Response to Child Marketing," *Journal of Advertising Research,* 17:6, December 1977.
48. Gladys G. Jenkins, "Families, Mass Communication and the Marketplace," *Childhood Education,* 54:2, November–December 1977.
49. C. C. Anderson and T. O. Maguire, "The Effect of TV Viewing on the Educational Performance of Elementary School Children," *Alberta Journal of Educational Research,* 24:3, September 1978.
50. Jackie Busch, "Television Effects on Reading: A Case Study," *Phi Delta Kappan,* 59:10, June 1978.
51. Steven H. Chaffee and Albert R. Tims, "Communicating Patterns and Adolescents' Television Viewing Behavior: A Study of the Influence of the Family and of Peers," *Fersehen und Bildung,* 11:3, 1977.
52. Wilbur Schramm, *Television in the Lives of Our Children,* Stanford University Press, Stanford, Calif., 1961.
53. Gary M. Ingersoll, "Sesame Street Can't Handle All the Traffic," *Phi Delta Kappan,* 53:3, November 1971.
54. Lynette K. Friedrich and Aletha H. Stein, "Prosocial Television and Young Children: The Effects of Verbal Labeling and Role-Playing on Learning and Behavior," *Child Development,* 46:1, March 1975.
55. John Van Hoose, "TV, The Effective 'Aide' for Affective Education," *Phi Delta Kappan,* 59:10, June 1978.
56. Priscilla Vail, *The World of the Gifted Child,* Walker & Co, New York, 1979.
57. E. Paul Torrance, "Helping Gifted Children Through Mental Health Information and Concepts," *Gifted Child Quarterly,* vol. II, Spring 1967.
58. Gina Ginsberg, "Homework with the Gifted and Talented Child: Practical Hints for Parents of Gifted Children," in *Parentspeak on Gifted and Talented Children,* Ventura County Superintendent of Schools Office, Ventura, Calif., January 1976.

4

School and Other Heartaches

I can't even recall when the subject of school became such a trauma for me. But after talking with other parents of GCs, I am certain our experiences were all quite similar.

Your child's first few years can be a very cozy existence: trips to the petting zoo, long discussions over the philosophical and spiritual ramifications of *The Velveteen Rabbit,* maybe even a window garden.

There are those parents and educators who devoutly believe that no school is better than a rotten school. And furthermore, all schools are rotten. "Deschooling,"[1] a concept first popularized by Ivan Illich, maintains that literate, loving parents, siblings and friends can provide the best educational environment for any child.

But most of us are too bound to our own academic indoctrinations to feel comfortable with that. Even if we ourselves were "horrible students," we at least had the feeling that being a "good student" was somehow better. Frankly, I don't have enough guts to yank my kid out of society. So school was, and is, a given.

When the subject first arose, I was amusingly naïve. School? What school? The best, of course, but what's that? Are there schools that specialize in gifted education? Will my GC have to clean erasers while the other children learn to read? Do I want him to skip grades? (My mother skipped the seventh grade and claims to have missed fractions and the hormonal maturation of her girlhood friends.)

Every parent has pangs of separation when that kid with the milk moustache climbs up into a bus driven by some un-known-but-suspected maniac. I think we can be forgiven for the preliminary judgment that "those fools down at the school don't know what they're doing." Unfortunately for the parents of a GC, these prejudicial thoughts often come true.

For the lucky parents, a very special school can perform according to plan:

Mr. and Mrs. Florenza:
We were at first concerned over Freddie's tendency to drift into coma and ignore the teacher's instructions. In the cafeteria, he was observed trading chocolate chip cookies for carrot sticks and offering copies of his math homework for the crusts of sandwiches.

When he entered the junior high art competition with a collage entitled "Barf Break," our suspicions were confirmed. After extensive discussion with and evaluation by our guidance counselor, Miss Direction, we have placed Freddie in the honors track of the Gifted Arts Program.

You are cordially invited to the first annual GAP exhibition, Monday October 14, at 7:30 P.M.

Sincerely,

Your Principal

It may be a bright, dedicated teacher who first identifies your GC as such. Your GC may be enrolled in one of the pioneering school systems that has taken on the challenges of providing the special education she needs. If so, you may reread Chapter 3, turn immediately to Chapter 5 or advance token to Boardwalk. For the rest of us, the agonizing decisions over "School, school, who's got the school?" can take a great deal of energy and bore a great many dinner guests.

I believe the first step toward a school decision is to carefully examine your own goals and priorities. The biggest problem parents face when choosing a school is an understanding of their own expectations.

Some parents have a hidden agenda when they set about to select a school. They want their GC to grow up to be the "best" and they have a very specific definition of just what being the best means. We've all seen basic psychology discussed on Merv Griffin, so I won't bore you with my amaturish attempts at analysis. But ask yourself if the goals you set for the education of your GC are the ones that would really be best for her, or if they are only the ones that sound good when said out loud. Have you placed yourself in a position of being parent, philosopher and prophet? Do you expect to make educational choices for a five-year-old that will shape the way in which that child adapts to society twenty to thirty years hence? Will you choose a school that emphasizes achievement through the "discipline" of education? Will you choose a school that offers a "free-to-explore" environment based upon a child's internal quest for knowledge?

These questions can become quite a burden. As you go about the important business of selecting a school, remember:

1. Any decision should be based upon the best information you can gather. Make it your task to research the schools available to you. Talk with warm and breathing teachers. The school's admissions officer or guidance counselor may lead a perfectly splendid tour, rattle off all the appropriate answers and still have nothing to do with the daily business of educating your child.

2. Ask your child what he wants and expects from the school. He may not know all the educational terminology, but your GC can most certainly tell you (by word and example) what kind of environment helps him learn.

An example: You observe at your four-year-old's preschool the day the class is making valentines. Your little GC has to be constantly reminded of the task at hand. The other children are busily cutting red hearts and she's running to the window to watch the Dempster Dumpster. The other children are lovingly pasting heart to paper doily and your GC tells the teacher she can't find the paste, or that her fingers are sore. After lots of patience and firm guidance, she finishes her project. Later that night (after you've promised to be surprised), you're presented with the creation. She glows as you swoon and smile and lovingly praise. She's proud that the valentine earns an immediate place of honor on the refrigerator door. For weeks, she points it out to every household guest. Perhaps (notice the "perhaps," because I really don't know her that well) your GC needs a "structured" approach to education—one in which certain tasks are required of her and little quarter is given.

Or, you observe that your five-year-old has already developed the orderly habits of your mother-in-law. Each morning, he carefully selects his projects for the day, assembles materials and sets to independent work. Much to your amazement, he will later return all tools to their proper places. You receive only a glare as you interrupt to tell him that dinner's on the table. Perhaps your GC would be more comfortable in a school environment where he is free to explore and march to his own bagpipe. He may need to be in a school where the bells don't ring every fifty minutes.

3. Keep an open mind and prepare to be wrong. Any school selection must be made with the understanding that it will be monitored and modified. Schools change, the faculty changes, Lord knows that educational trends and philosophies change; so you'll have to be aware and adaptable at any time.

Accept the fact that in twelve to sixteen years your GC may look you in the face and tell you he should have been sent to the School for the Performing Arts. When this happens, you pat him on the back, give him the phone number of the nearest community theater and promise to come opening night. It's never too late to learn a new skill.

4. Don't be lulled into complacency by a poorly constructed school system. Administrators of these systems will tell you that they have a special program for GCs: in the third grade they're given enrichment classes. Your GC needs immediate and constant special education *now*, not a little in the third grade and then an independent study period in high school.

A PRIMER IN EDUCATIONAL PHILOSOPHIES

Step number two is to coordinate your beliefs and expectations with a specific philosophy of education. Despite the verbosity of professional literature, educational philosophies can be type-cast easily:

"Sit at your desk" (traditional didactic)
"Discover a desk" (Americanized Montessori and subsequent clones)
"Build a desk" (vocational/technical)
"So who needs a desk?" (open concept)

Superimposed over a school's basic orientation will be the personal commitments and style of each individual teacher. Teaching styles can be classified as follows:

"I'm the teacher, so I've got the biggest desk."
"My desk is in the other room, but I can get it if I need it."
"You can sit at my desk to see if it fits you."
"Let's all sit in a circle and relate."

The possibilities are multitudinous. You can, therefore, find a classroom with the formula: "Discover your own desk—but mine is bigger," or "Let's all sit in a circle and talk about how you need to get in your desk." When selecting a school for your GC, you must never forget the delicate interweaving of a school's philosophy with an individual teacher's ability.

THE PRIVATE/PUBLIC DICHOTOMY

There is a commonly held assumption that expensive, independent and/or restrictive private schools can offer much more in terms of gifted education than can the public school system. After all, proponents maintain, the public schools are fulfilling their primary objective: they provide general, appropriate education for the masses. (And of course, [(Curt, Jane, Alvin] is above that throng.)

It is most difficult to determine the validity of this belief. But when we hear of the high school graduates unable to read on an eighth-grade level, it seems to be undeniably correct. Nevertheless, private schools often have the financial advantage of quality PR, and none of us should underestimate the importance of a good hype job. If the school's literature is printed on rag paper; if the admissions director is polite (albeit "properly distant"); if the facility is opulent with resources and the kids all wear designer jeans, it really is hard to separate actual academic standards from perceived academic standards. (And as Henry Kissinger so skillfully reminded us, sometimes the perception of truth is as important as truth itself.)

The same veils are present in a less-traditional/alternative school. Just because they put raisins and carob drops in the vending machines, just because the teachers "can-really-relate-to-the-space-you're-coming-from," doesn't mean they know how to teach your kid.

I've concluded that one way to preevaluate any school may be to:

Spend time observing the in-class behavior of the teacher assigned to your GC.

Seek the opinions of disgruntled parents who left the school.

Seek the opinions of parents who are thrilled with the school.

Ask to see some specific lesson plans and student evaluation models.

Talk to some students in the school.

Add it up, divide by 0.4 and see what you've got left.

I don't care where you go, you will most often find private schools to be one of three genres:

Our Town's Country Day (OTCD).
Our Lady of Perpetual Attentiveness.
Berries of the Field.

Our Town's Country Day has the reputation of being "the top," "the crème de la crème," "the best" that money can buy.

Either admission standards are high, or they require only that you have to be breathing, devoid of educational handicaps, and bankrolled. The students are presented as the kind of children you would want your child to know. (You could retire on the Izod concession alone.) The faculty is poised, polished and a credit to any profession. The physical plant is superbe. (Note the extra "e.") You will be assured that members of the faculty attended such institutions as Rutgers, Yale, the Sorbonne, Harvard, Amherst and Smith. (Ever wonder where all those graduates went?) The school always strives "to establish an environment of academic and developmental excellence" and "helps establish values significant to the cultural, social and intellectual maturation of responsible citizens."

We were once considering a company transfer and found it necessary to apply to schools in several cities. One of the most hideous experiences occurred when I took our GC to his admissions test at an OTCD. What we had been led to believe was a personal interview turned into group testing of thirty potential junior kindergartners and a lesson in marketing theatrics. We parents were led off on a spin through the empty corridors while our prodigies were marched into a classroom to meet Mrs. Tattersall. I peeked over thirty little heads in parade dress to see thirty little desks, thirty little test papers, thirty number 2 pencils and big Mrs. Tattersall. (Later, after much pumping and a McDonald's Happy Meal, my GC described what turned out to be the Boehm Test of Picture Concepts—erroneously given as a group test, I might add.)

After the tour, the parents were properly herded into the lower school library to sweat out the examinations. I haven't seen so much tension since the Cuban Missile Crisis.

"We're fully prepared to place Brent in another school if he isn't accepted." (Brent was probably the one who wrote all over our son's back.)

"My husband has made it perfectly clear to his company that we will not transfer to this state if Garrett isn't accepted to OTCD!" (Could we be so lucky?)

As the parent-proctor returned to tell us the ordeal was over, I ventured a question regarding the educational philosophy of the school. I was told that the Director of Admissions would be happy to discuss any questions with the parents of those children accepted for attendance. Presumably, the rest of us could go eat an eraser. Outside Mrs. Tattersall's, the scene of reunion must have been what it was when the trains brought evacuated children back into postwar London. I found my GC, turned on my heel, and we escaped with our lives.

Our Lady of Perpetual Attentiveness is representative of the parochial or religious-affiliated schools of any spiritual persuasion. If you are committed to a specific religious doctrine, these schools can provide you with the peace of mind that your GC is receiving an education in keeping with your beliefs.

It's difficult to criticize a parochial school without fear of offending someone's religion. That is certainly not my intention. (After all, I still have to live with my relatives.) But while some may openly encourage the exchange of cultural and social ideals, the parochial schools I have personally seen were educationally dogmatic.

I remember St. Markowitz. St. Markowitz boasted a junior kindergarten in which four-year-olds were systematically, methodically and with great order taught to read.

When I asked about the program, I was told, "We believe in basic education, corporal punishment and sound American principles. That's the St. Markowitz way."

When I asked about individual attention, I was told, "The children all learn together at the same pace. That's the St. Markowitz way."

When I asked about addressing each child's special needs, I was told: "That's all incorporated in the St. Markowitz way."

Maybe their way will work for some. And if I ever meet a basically educated, sound American corporal, I'll know he probably went to St. Markowitz. Personally, I couldn't send my kid to a school that would eventually have kicked his mother out on her proverbial posterior.

Berries of the Field is often billed as an alternative to traditional education. When you talk with the school staff, they will stress freedom of choice, inner discipline, sunshine and a comfortable school wardrobe.

They can be completely sincere about respecting others and the free exchange of values. Racial prejudices are nonexistent, and an active attempt will be made to introduce your child to other cultures and societies. Economic differences are deplored, and each child is told of egalitarian ethics. But don't ever try sending your kid to school with a bologna sandwich and a Twinkie. Such openmindedness rarely extends to processed foods, big cars or Saturday morning cartoons. Our son was always being asked what he had for breakfast. The day he answered "pancakes and Coke" we got a call regarding his hyperactivity and a lecture on the merits of protein-based meals.

They will tell you that every child has a gift and that he must be the one to determine how that gift is to be expressed. Students will decide their own curricula, academic requirements and evaulation methods, usually in a contract of some kind or another.

Berries of the Field will most probably tout an interpretation of either the open concept or the Montessori method of education. The "open" part supposedly refers to both the physical and the philosophical aspects of the program. Early devotees of open education thought of traditional classrooms as being little boxes that functionally and spiritually limit learning. Therefore, the classroom walls in an open-concept school are free-flowing and/or nonexistent.

When implemented according to theory, open schools can be a blend of active learning and informality. Discipline is certainly present, but often it is a more constructive and self-motivated control mechanism. At their worst, open schools appear to be and *are* chaotic lessons in the absurd: children running around with little internal or external direction and teachers who seem unable or unwilling to tie together assorted events and discoveries. Perhaps the biggest handicap for this type of school is the fact that most of us still regard education as something with immediately observable and quantitatively measurable results. The open system asks us to suspend these traditions for less apparent, more abstract indications of a child's growth.

In *Open Education and the American School,* Dr. Roland Barth has remarked: "It is not surprising then, that most parents view open classrooms as a risky, untried experiment with their children."[2]

Our experience with an open class admittedly was brief. The children were encouraged to select their own activities, time schedules and achievement levels. Our GC would always make the conscious, intrinsically motivated, self-directed, internally determined, free decision to spend the day on the playground. I'll admit that I panicked. Given a few more months or a year, he might have tired of that and explored the other and perhaps more substantive elements of education. The December day he "chose" to spend in a freezing drizzle, I "chose" to find a new school.

A Humble Tribute to Dr. Maria Montessori

So much has been done in the name of Dr. Maria Montessori that she must truly be regarded as an educational revolutionary. Her story is something out of Twentieth Century-Fox. As a young physician in the slums of Rome, she took upon herself the task of educating those children discarded because of retardation, physical handicaps and learning disorders. She theorized that all humans strive to bring order out of chaos. Her methods involved a prepared, orderly environment that allowed each child to discover truth and thus education.

She was one of the first educators to recognize the value of intrinsic (or self-)motivation. She believed that in order for learning to take place, the teacher should be a resource, rather than a dictator. Her philosophy stressed teaching young children the skills of concentration, tenacity, thoroughness and self-confidence. These, she believed, were the building blocks for subsequent, more "formalized" learning.[3]

Perhaps her primary contributions to education were:

1. Observations that the young child mentally absorbs her environment.
2. An emphasis upon the link between tactile stimulation and learning. This concept (based upon earlier work by Dr. Edouard Seguin) is represented by the cutout sandpaper letters that allow children to "feel the alphabet" in order to learn it.
3. The separation of learning tasks into simple, easily identifiable steps.

4. The concept of allowing a child to see some progress re-
gardless of overall success or failure.

Although she was concerned with the young student, her
learning model has been applied to every level of education.
And Montessori concepts are now an assumption of virtually
all modern practices of early childhood education. This most
certainly includes special education for the gifted.

Much that is *not* "Montessori" is also done in her name. If
you are considering a Montessori learning experience for your
2½-to-6-year-old, be certain that the school is endorsed by
either the American Montessori Society or the Association
Montessori Internationale. Also, there are dozens of books telling you how to create a Montessori environment in your own
home.

With regard to private schools in general, I've obviously expressed the extremes. (And maybe even taken some cheap
shots.) Each of these schools can, under proper direction and a
dedicated faculty, be excellent centers of learning. We have had
several negative experiences, but our GC is currently enrolled
in a cooperative effort involving two fantastic schools. (The
first is a university-sponsored program for GCs and the second
is a heterogeneous private school.) It is because of these positive experiences that I probably speak with some smugness.

When confronting the public/private dichotomy, you can
quickly become consumed with two basic questions: (1) What is
the best method for guiding your child's abilities? and (2) What
is available to you on this very day? Answers to these questions
rarely present themselves as clear and present alternatives.
Rather, they are interwoven in a confusing clump of facts, figures and fantasy.

The question of choosing the best from what is available
usually gets immediate attention. Obviously it is a decision that
must be made in the context of many outside factors:

- How far are you willing/able to commute?
- Can you afford tuition to a private school if the public
  school is deemed inappropriate? If you scrape up the

money, will your GC be the school's financial and social waif—unable to spend Christmas in Switzerland or tour China during spring break? Does it matter?

- Can you move to a city with an excellent public school system?
- Are you in a mobile career that necessitates frequent relocation?
- Are you completely dependent upon the decisions made in the office of the principal, or do you have a voice at the school board meetings?
- Do you have a specific religious and/or political orientation that you want incorporated into your child's education?

Private schools have traditionally offered options to those parents able to afford them. But public school systems now recognize the need to provide alternative educational modes. In many large cities, you can select a school according to educational philosophy rather than according to geography. This new flexibility allows the parent of a GC to make some active choices even when the system provides no special education for the gifted and talented.

WHY DO GCs NEED SPECIAL EDUCATION?

When the parents of a child with limited vision ask for textbooks in large type, no one even whispers disagreement. And that's as it should be. Apart from the legality,* it seems universally correct. However, the parents of a GC asking for special education can expect to hear, "What makes you think your kid deserves something special?"

Gifted education is no more complicated than "teaching toward" each child's potential. If Karla is reading on the average

---

* Public Law 94-142, often referred to as the "Bill of Rights for the Handicapped," stipulates that appropriate public education must be available for all children *and* that parents must be included in the development of Individual Education Plans (IEP) for each child's special needs. It is through P.L. 94-142 that many programs in special education for GCs have been initiated.

seventh-grade level while only in the third grade, she is given seventh-grade reading material. If Jane is capable of comprehending calculus, she is not forced to sit through eighth-grade mathematics. If Brad loves to sketch horses, why must he wait until the entire class is scheduled to take art?

When discussing gifted education, we have to take it step by step: (1) Do they need it? (2) Are they getting it? (3) If not, then why? (4) What is it anyway?

Do They Need It?

Apparently some of them don't. Some GCs are so talented that they can survive dull and repetitive school tasks, out-think incompetent materials, thrive in self-directed independent study, play the games and emerge with some semblance of their original intelligence and creativity. Maybe one or two students out of every high school graduation will make it. You guess what happens to the rest.

In "The Education of Children with High Mental Ability," James Dunlap has said, "By the time they enter school, gifted children are advanced from one to four years or more in capacity to learn."[4] They already know the alphabet and basic geometric shapes. Some already know how to read. Many can solve basic mathematical problems, speak impromptu or cut and paste with aplomb. GCs very often relate well in social situations, respond positively to instruction and attend to tasks. That just about covers every social and academic goal of almost every kindergarten and first grade throughout this country.

So what about the GCs who enter school with these skills? Do you think they all patiently sit with stoic silence and angelic smiles? Wrong! Instead they may mix the green paint with the snack juice, impale a classmate with a number rod or relieve themselves on the shrubbery. Obviously school can't be one continuous trip to Disney World, but spending nine months of your life watching other children discover what you already know can be very frustrating. How many times can one person learn the colors in the rainbow?

We see the evidence of inappropriate education for the GC

in all too many ways. When school is not a stimulating environment, GCs will become restless, inattentive, apathetic or disruptive. Barely surviving the dreary dull days, they can come to complain about doing any schoolwork. They lose the will to struggle against the system.

One pathetic statistic school administrators often use to defend a lack of gifted education is the evidence that somewhere near the fourth grade the IQ and achievement scores of heretofore GCs seem to diminish. They call it a "leveling off" of developmental traits. Leveling off is not a physical law of nature. As with muscle tissue, intellectual ability can atrophy when not exercised. Moreover, many GCs come to feel that when little is expected of them, little is necessary. Professor John Gowan, former director of the National Association for Gifted Children, believes that this leveling off is merely an indication of the tragedy that occurs when GCs go unchallenged. Eventually, frustration and social pressures to conform to group achievement levels take their toll. The GCs simply "learn not to be so smart."[5] And I don't care what your mother said to get you to go to school, enduring boredom does not build character.

Some bored geniuses simply drop out of school. We know that our schools are losing GCs. There are, in fact, so many educational studies about the intellectual abilities of high school dropouts that I hardly know where to begin. As early as 1965, Pennsylvania school officials had learned that of the youth who dropped out of that state's public school systems (1964-65), 500 had standardized IQ scores of over 120, and eighty had IQs in excess of 130. Other studies show that from 8 to 11 percent of all high school dropouts have scored 110 or above on standardized IQ tests.[6]

Some GCs develop sloppy and inaccurate work habits. In order to passively resist the system, they often rush through school tasks, just to be "done with it." They can be poor in spelling, careless in handwriting and inaccurate in arithmetic.*

---

* Some experts believe that GCs generally exhibit sloppy handwriting because their thoughts come faster than the physical ability to write. Typing is now used in many gifted programs. It seems particularly useful for gifted preschoolers/early-schoolers who lack the fine motor dexterity essential for readable penmanship.

And in severe cases of undermotivation, they become lackadaisical in completing or handing in assignments.

Many GCs prefer to say "I don't know" rather than to recite information already completely understood. Imagine yourself if our society required you to recite the alphabet each time you sat down to read. Or what if every time you bought something, you had to tell the clerk the name of the President pictured on the one dollar bill. Trust me—you would soon tire of the routine. Dunlap calls it the "revolt against rote." He says that this rejection of material unworthy of her attention is the GC's unconscious way of retaining self-respect.[7] ("Look, I know it's George Washington, but I'll be damned if I tell you one more time!")

Other GCs hide abilities so as not to be assigned extra work. Teacher: "Why, Freddie, you've finished all your math problems; (just for that) ... here are twenty more to do." As we used to say in junior high, "I may not be smart, but I'm sure not dumb."

None of this is big news to anyone who has bothered to pay attention. In 1938, Leta Hollingworth studied GCs and concluded that those with IQs of 140 or more needed one-half of the time to complete regular school assignments as did normal children; those with IQs over 170 needed one-fourth as much time; children with IQs of 180 and more scarcely needed to be in school at all because they already knew so much of the required information.[8]

No one being of sound mind would suggest that GCs cannot derive some benefit from normal school experiences. Socialization, conversation, culturalization, a sense of morality and mortality—these acquirements are essential if the GC is to become a functioning member of society. But when a child is completely mired down in a system of what is, to her, mere "busy work," other and more negative traits can be nurtured: avoidance, manipulation, apathy, hostility and total distrust of authority. After all, if teachers are omnipotent—and they are the ones in charge—the GC may wonder why they can't catch on to the fact that something is wrong.

Are They Getting It?

The current light upon special education for the gifted was ignited by a 1971 report by Sidney Marland, U.S. Commissioner of Education. Reflecting upon an earlier ignition point in the drive to establish gifted education in America, Marland now implores the Russian government to "Send Up More Sputnicks." He says, "Sputnick changed the face of education in America. It jarred us out of an unjustified complacency with the quality of our schools...."[9]

Unlike other forms of special education, gifted education is not protected by a federal blanket. Federal monies are available to school systems ($6.28 million in 1981), but public education in this country remains by and large under the jurisdiction of the states. In fact, 80 percent of federal funds are now given directly to the states with 90 percent of that being directed through local school districts.[10]

Those states with major state funding (1978–79) for gifted education are North Carolina ($31 million), Pennsylvania ($18 million), California ($13.4 million), Florida ($13 million), Georgia ($6 million), Connecticut ($3.8 million) and Illinois ($3.6 million). Several others have allocated token funds to "research the professional literature" or "prepare an analysis for consideration." This is in light of the estimated $10 billion that was spent on all public education during the same time period.

Those states with major funding provided researchers from the U.S. Office of Gifted and Talented with the following data regarding the distribution of those funds:[11]

	Projected total number of gifted students in state	Percentage of gifted students served
North Carolina	Information not available	Information not available
Pennsylvania	70,000	68
California	180,000	89
Florida	31,000	2
Georgia	30,000	80
Connecticut	63,200	14
Illinois	111,906	59

If Not, Then Why?

I can't answer the question why not? I wish that I could.
Harold Lyon, Director of the U.S. Office of Education for
Gifted and Talented, wrote in 1972, "It is paradoxical that in a
time of widespread concern for the waste and destruction of
water, air and land, we are wasting through neglect, the very
natural resources that might do most to help improve the quality of our culture and assure strong leadership for the future."[12]

On the surface, it seems to be a simple matter of money. If
there were plenty to go around, we're told, GCs would most
certainly be given special education. "But meanwhile, would
you want us to take the Braille typewriters from a school for
the blind?" we're asked by school administrators. "Would you
want us to stop helping the mentally retarded gain dignity and
self-reliance?" Maybe the real weakness of GCs is that nobody
really thinks they're handicapped.

There has been a long-fought controversy over whether or
not the GC is technically handicapped in our public school systems. The U.S. Office of the Gifted and Talented is administra-
tively housed in the Bureau of Education of the Handicapped.
Twenty-seven states now include gifted education in their departments of Special Education for the Handicapped.[13] And
until recent years, most educational literature regarding the
gifted was included as chapter inserts in textbooks on "exceptional" or handicapped students.

The opponents of the labeling say it is misleading and detrimental. Proponents say that inappropriate education is in itself
an educational handicap. And still others say that riding the
legislative coattails of the handicapped is the most practical
way of obtaining desperately needed funding; thus their advice
is, "Shut up and take the money." Probably the most confused
by the label are the GCs themselves. They often have a hard
time understanding why superior ability should be considered a
"handicap," particularly when no one has yet to throw them a
telethon.

Meanwhile, educators in programs for the mentally and
physically disadvantaged—including the gifted—have to

scramble for financial crumbs while school systems in America finance whirlpool saunas for varsity football teams, construct basketball cathedrals or color-coordinate the baseball socks. Perhaps a more realistic weakness is that neither the handicapped nor the majority of GCs fill the stadiums and thrill the crowds. (Gotta sell that popcorn!)

What Is It Anyway?

And why all the fuss over education for the gifted? After you've reviewed the educational alternatives available to your GC, you're ready to compare them to the "state of the art."

A few innovative educators have been studying the ways in which our schools have been squandering talent. Therefore, those of us who advocate special education for the gifted are able to have something quite specific in mind. But first: I can't talk to you about philosophies of gifted education until we get something settled about learning theory.

Simply having information, no matter how relevant, pass in the general vicinity of your body will not ensure learning. (I had a high school teacher who used to say, "You kids aren't gonna learn this stuff by sittin' on it.") That statement sounds so obvious as to be absurd. And yet, educators and parents often act as if they thought the reverse were true. Adam took a class in American history. In fact, Adam received an "A" in said class. Therefore, Adam should know the names of the original thirteen colonies.

Earlier, I mentioned Bloom's Taxonomy. In order for a lesson to be learned, he concluded, it must be:

1. Evaluated by the student. (Some are merely heard.)
2. Synthesized into "core" or relevant material. (It could be pure memorization here.)
3. Analyzed with regard to past experiences, beliefs, commitments, etc. (It's very easy to fake assimilation: "Oh yeah, I understand exactly what you mean.")
4. Applied to a real experience. (I took a high school physics lab, but the boys did the experiments and the girls kept the labbooks.)
5. Remembered.

Even after step 2, many students can regurgitate information and score well on tests. GCs (and I *am* coming to a point) are often either (1) so skillful at steps 1 to 3 that they fool parents and teachers into thinking they know how to apply and remember information, or (2) so adept at stages 4 and 5 that they don't bore themselves or impress us with steps 1 to 3. The first GC gets an A+ in Physics and can't explain the theory of aerodynamics. The second student gets a D in Physics and later builds her own hang glider. (There is, of course, the student who gets a C in physics, never heard of aerodynamics and lands a job designing military aircraft, but that's another book.)

Forgive me for a personal anecdote here. In the early sixties, I was a part of an experiment in gifted education conducted by the National Science Foundation. Then a high school sophomore, I took a course in college-level biology. (Others studied mathematics, physics and chemistry.) Two years later, the university where I enrolled as a freshman wouldn't admit me to the required general biology course. It did make sense. Because I'd already taken that course, I was registered in a microbiology class. At the end of the semester, I had the second highest grade average in the group. The professor told me I was the only nonbiology, nonpremedical major ever to score an A in the course. Do I know anything about microbiology today? Can I name one single amino acid? Should I have studied to become a doctor? A resounding "no" to all three.

With regard to learning, GCs can easily be misinterpreted and thus misled by teachers and parents alike. I believe that this factor represents a fundamental way in which existing school systems waste the skills of the gifted and talented.

AND NOW—ON TO WHAT WE WANT

There are currently three educational approaches most often used to guide the learning processes of GCs: enrichment, ability grouping and acceleration.

Enrichment

An educational concept as ancient as recess and chalkboards, enrichment is of three types:

Horizontal—more work at the same level. Many teachers unsophisticated in the techniques of gifted education resort to horizontal enrichment, probably out of pure frustration. "Jennifer is so bright in algebra; I've given her twenty-five additional problems so she'll not be bored."

Vertical—increased complexity. Without question, vertical enrichment is the preferred method. "Jennifer is so bright in algebra; I thought she would enjoy some problems in computer logic."

Goodies—glee club, a field trip to the bakery, a guest speaker from India. Goodies are most often recited to parents who ask a school administrator about gifted education. "Why of course we have gifted education: we have band, art classes, the science club, the pom-pomettes...." All children benefit from goodies; but in themselves, they *are not* gifted education.

Dr. Joseph Renzulli, Director of the Teaching the Talented Program, University of Connecticut, has proposed a model from which many gifted enrichment programs have been cloned. As is true about innovators in general, experts seem either to dismiss Renzulli as a loony-tune or applaud him as the greatest thing since cracked ice.

Very simply stated (and I hate to paraphrase Renzulli because his writing is such enjoyable reading), the Enrichment Triad consists of three interrelated activities: (1) general exploratory groups, (2) group training and (3) small-group investigations of real problems. The first two would probably be helpful to all children. Objectives are to develop thinking and feeling, and to expand interests. It is the third activity that he finds so essential for GCs. In this model, the students have complete freedom to pursue any topic, at whatever depth, and through any feasible method they desire.

The teacher's role is threefold: (1) to provide assistance in the identification of, and focus on, solvable problems, (2) to find resources, (3) to find appropriate outlets for the products of discovery. Thus, Renzulli stresses that the teacher is to provide for the systematic development of the learning process. He does not advocate (as some critics charge) a capricious dabbling into every conceivable topic. Once a student has selected a topic for study—once he has selected his method—the teacher should help him develop his skills of inquiry.[14]

Teacher: "Well, yes, Brian, I can certainly see where you're coming from with the photon/meson thing; but have you considered how you will obtain access to a linear accelerator?"

These enrichment groups are to be run concurrently with, but in addition to, a "regular" school curriculum. (It seems this is the key factor for dubious school board members.) Students come in and out of the triad as their interests coincide with the group's activities. Critics call this the "revolving door" approach: a student decides to be gifted today in urban development, gifted next week in baroque music—next semester, gifted in nothing.

Meanwhile, back home again in Indiana, there's more to Purdue than the Boilermakers. Dr. John Feldhusen is a professor at Purdue and the director of "Super Saturday." Parents in my small Indiana community pack up their GCs and drive 3½ hours to participate in this enrichment program. When asked why they went to such lengths to put their kids in the Saturday morning classes, one parent replied, "It beats the hell out of 'Plastic Man and Scooby-Do Meet the Super Friends.'"

Feldhusen works with two groups of GCs (110–140 IQ or 60th–80th percentile scores and 140+ IQ or 90th percentile scores) in the areas of math, science, language arts and social studies.

In his three-stage model, GCs progress through:

1. Basic convergent and divergent thinking vis-à-vis creative thinking games lead by a teacher.
2. Complex creative problem solving, with the teacher as a resource.
3. Independent research to define and clarify a problem, gather data and communicate results. For example: students may decide to write a play, develop a news program, plan a city of the future or plan the solution to a community problem.

Feldhusen believes all gifted education should have goals similar to those of each Super Saturday course:

To develop thinking skills
To develop positive self-concepts
To develop intellectual abilities
To develop independence[15]

Any inquiries regarding Super Saturday should be sent to:

Super Saturday Program
Gifted Education Resource Institute
Purdue University, SCC-G
West Lafayette, IN 47907

Ability Grouping

Ability grouping is a pragmatic footpath that has grown up into a philosophical quagmire. Somewhere in the early dawn of education, a teacher learned that if you had a group of children with diverse levels of understanding in any subject, you could better serve them all if you would first divide the group according to ability.

"Okay, all you readers, over there in the corner—take your books. All you nonreaders, up here at the chalkboard."

It seemed idyllic in its simplicity. The children who knew basic math could work on algebra, and the children who didn't could work on number recognition and the relationships of primary units. Who among us can't remember the redbirds and the bluebirds?

Suddenly, ability grouping brings terror to the hearts of those who fear it will cause an intellectually elite class. They argue that separating GCs from other children will give GCs a "superior attitude" and deprive normal children of the opportunity to learn from GCs.

In brief, a rebuttal: It seems to me that if a GC is enrolled in a school system where she is continually underchallenged, never required to crack a book and still able to score A's, this is a place where she can truly nurture an attitude of superiority.

As the parent of a child who has participated in a homogeneous class of GCs, I can point to some real advantages:

He was able to see that he was not alone in his interests, drives and abilities.

He was able to see that there were, in fact, others in the world with superior abilities.

He was able to more fully realize his own superior abilities.

I think this last point is an important one. We can go overboard in expecting the GC to assume a posture of total equalitarianism and/or humility. He needs to understand that his particular capabilities are not "gifted" upon us all. More importantly, he needs to learn how to handle that fact and make some real decisions about what (if anything) he intends to do about it.

In regard to depriving other children of learning opportunities, the truth is that GCs—particularly the extremely brilliant ones—can intimidate the normal or slow student of *the same chronological age.* Furthermore, it seems absurd that rational adults who spent four to six years in university instruction on the art of teaching suddenly decide that a bright student can be a naturally facilitating instructor for children with other special learning needs. And while a little tutoring service may be good for the soul, I have serious questions about the ways in which GCs are often exploited as volunteer teachers' aides *at the expense* of their own development. (This tirade does not apply to those situations where GCs act as mentors to younger GCs of similar ability levels.)

Acceleration

Acceleration is one big question mark in most of our minds. Many of us have parents, aunts or uncles who were accelerated for all kinds of vague or obscure reasons. Grade skipping, early school admission or advancement through summer school may have once been linked to the practicality of helping those you can and getting the others into the labor force or off to war. As a bonus, it was easy and required no additional capital expenditure. ("Harold, you'll be going to Mrs. Rosencamp's sixth grade from now on.")

After the postwar baby boom, school systems began to shudder with bulging kindergartens. Early admission to the first grade was commonly recommended as the easiest and most favorable means of acceleration or grade skipping.[16] I, for one, entered the first grade at five rather than six years, and my friend Susan did too. Susan was eventually our high school valedictorian, and the last I heard, she had a Ph.D. in psychology.

Sometime in the late 1950s, the psychologists began telling parents that acceleration was creating social misfits. Suddenly, the educators were down on it too. They cautioned that children pushed into older peer groups could be overwhelmed by pressures to conform to "sociological situations beyond their maturation thresholds." (This just meant they might have a hard time getting dates or be embarrassed in phys ed showers.)

I can understand why teachers resist acceleration. They see all the failures. It's like the doctor who scares you to death with all the remote complications of a relatively minor surgery because she's seen a couple of "close ones." This is of little comfort to the parents of a GC. When you have a six-year-old who reads on the third-grade level, your gut reaction is that she's going to go crazy with Dick and Jane.

Antiacceleration educators will tell you that even though she should be given supplementary reading material on the third-grade level, your daughter also needs to experience the emotional cross-pollination that occurs when first graders read together. Oddly enough, that's the same argument used by advocates of commercial television viewing. How can a child relate to his peers in the idiom of his generation if he doesn't know Ponch from Jon? (They're a little like Punch and Judy, but different.)

On Being Gifted is a collection of the thoughts and opinions of twenty high gifted students. In it, a fifteen-year-old college sophomore is quoted, ". . . it seems that one's social level follows, more or less, from one's intellectual level. I cannot substantiate that, except that my experience has shown this to be true."

And from a student who decided not to skip the senior year of high school: "Why? I'm not mature enough. I think I need another year to work out a balance between expressing my feelings and tactfully shutting up when necessary."[17] (I often feel that way myself.)

When you have an eighth-grader who has been conducting independent research on geothermal energy sources, those high school physics labs can look pretty appealing. Antiacceleration educators, however, will tell you that the misunderstanding of complex concepts often occurs when students skip over the basic levels. This argument is also touted to budding artists. "Remember, before he became a creative genius, Picasso mastered the craft of his forerunners." (That concept still strikes me as either a logical falsehood or an illogical truth.)

And then, enter Julian Stanley of the Study of Mathematically Precocious Youth (SMPY) and Johns Hopkins University. The SMPY seems to "fly in the face" of all the antiaccelerationists. This project is based upon the (1) discovery, (2) description, and (3) development of precocious mathematics students. A fourth purpose has recently been added: the dissemination of this knowledge to other educators.

After several brazen talent hunts in the Mid-Atlantic states, the SMPY project has studied over 7000 GC and reached the following conclusions:

> So-called educational enrichment is not suitable for math-talented students unless it leads to subject matter and/or grade acceleration.
> It is unfortunate that accelerated options are unfairly ruled out by parents as well as educators from public and private schools.[18]

In reviewing the work at Johns Hopkins, Michael Wallach, professor of psychology, Duke University, has summarized Stanley's conclusions as follows: "Rather than believing we can teach people to become more 'intelligent' or more 'creative,' we should be teaching them as effectively as possible to master specific disciplines."[19] According to Wallach, Stanley shows us that the way to find effective teaching techniques is to examine closely the structure of the subject to be taught. (This would not go over big in many teachers' lounges. It means that they would have to throw away their used lesson plans and old college notes, rethink basic concepts and come up with something new for the 9:00 A.M. lecture.)

And so once again acceleration is being examined as a viable alternative for some GCs. John Feldhusen and Ann Wyman of Purdue's super-enrichment program conclude that enrichment is not enough: "When no other program or very limited programs are available in the schools, Super Saturday type programs can provide valuable instruction for the gifted. However, in the regular school setting, full scale programming for the gifted calls for a variety of offerings and for acceleration. Grade skipping is *often* desirable for gifted students who are far advanced in basic achievement areas."[20]

If acceleration (in both subject and grade) were an acceptable commonplace event, perhaps some of the fears about social and developmental maladjustment could be overcome. Most school systems assign students to cubbyholes (known as grade levels) solely on the basis of chronological age. Where is it written that only ten-year-olds can study the science projects assigned to the fourth year of elementary school? Why can't one or two or five eight-year-old GCs slip into fourth-grade science class? This is what the open-school advocates had in mind when they literally tore down classroom walls. (Actually, I know "why." Principals and counselors would have to spend more of their summers reworking the class schedules.)

Now that we've discussed the "big three" of gifted education (enrichment, ability grouping, acceleration), it's time to look at some random and very exciting ideas on the subject. While experts continue to disagree sincerely on the best type of gifted education, most authorities are in agreement that directive teaching (lecture) and memorization drills are the least effective approaches for GCs. What seems to run throughout the theories and techniques is the belief that GCs should be allowed to discover, explore, experiment and be encouraged to create new solutions rather than to regurgitate old answers.

Some experts insist that GCs should be taught to strive for long-term remote rewards and be weaned from immediate grat-

ifications. More moderate counsel suggests they be fed necessary and basic facts as soon and as quickly as possible through
such means as teaching machines and programmed learning.
Furthermore, they should be encouraged to utilize factual
storehouses (computers, calculators, dictionaries, logarithm
tables, etc.) so that they can be free to engage in high levels of
thinking.[21] Thus, we should not ask a GC to memorize the
countries of the world and their capitals when she can look that
up in any atlas. (After the African revolutions I found myself in
possession of such totally worthless information as the capital
city of the Belgian Congo and the colonial name for Chad.)

They are called "research and retrieval" skills and they
mean anything from being able to read the *Readers' Guide to
Periodical Literature* to knowing how to charm a reference librarian. These skills are the tools that can most help the GC.

I had a chemistry teacher who used to say, "The educated
man doesn't need to know everything, just where to find it." I
mentally carried that quote around until it occurred to me that
it was probably a paraphrase. I found that my teacher was expressing the thoughts of either Georg Simmel—"He is educated who knows where to find out what he doesn't know"—or
William Feather: "An education isn't how much you have committed to memory, or even how much you know. It's being able
to differentiate between what you know and what you don't.
It's knowing where to go to find out what you need to know;
and it's knowing how to use the information once you get it."[22]

Finding two such similar quotations naturally made me
wonder who had paraphrased whom. I discovered that Georg
Simmel (1858–1918), German sociologist and philosopher, was
one of the first social scientists to write on alienation and urban
stress. Several of his books are still in print, including *The
Problems of History: An Epistemological Essay* and *Conflict
and the Web of Group Affiliations* (definitely not your basic
poolside reading).[23]

William Feather proved much more interesting. He started
out as a reporter, spent some time with the National Cash Register Company and ended up in Cleveland with his own printing and publishing business. His quotation on education came

from *Business of Life* and a few of his publications were *Haystacks & Smokestakes, Ideals and Follies of Business* and *Talk about Women*.[24] (I wish I had been able to locate that one.) Feather is also credited with that great line: "We all find time to do what we really want to do."[25]

I never did find out who paraphrased whom. William Feather was twenty-nine years old when Georg Simmel died, so it is possible that Simmel paraphrased Feather. And publisher William Feather, Jr., told me that his father's thoughts and words were original. Nevertheless, you get the point of the exercise and I didn't see any sense in troubling Mr. Feather, Sr. (now ninety-one) with such trivia.

THEORY AND PRACTICE IN GIFTED EDUCATION TODAY

The application of most gifted educational programs is based upon two assumptions:

1. The brain is divided into two separately functioning hemispheres.
2. The intellect is an incredibly complex mechanism.

Hemispheres of the Brain

For over thirty years, we've accepted the fact that the brain is composed of two cerebral hemispheres that function quite independently. The right hemisphere is believed to be the cradle of creativity, while the left handles "mechanical" activities such as speech and other conscious cognition such as logic, analysis, vocabulary and knowledge of digits.

As you study gifted education, you will be bombarded with phrases such as right hemispheric imagery, stimulation of the right hemisphere (always presented as a positive goal), hemispheric lateralization, the role of hemisphericity, the inner space and the forgotten half. Educators love to drop this jargon as if everyone else knew what it meant. Don't be scared off by it all—it's easy to keep straight. Flush any old "political" stereotypes from your mind and think of the right side of the brain as being responsible for creative, innovative thought, and the left side of the brain as being responsible for the more traditionally academic qualities of logic, memory, etc.

The accepted belief is that traditional education has long ignored the right hemisphere. For a more in-depth look into the subject, I would suggest:

> *Understanding the Alpha Child at Home and School,* by Fadely and Hosler; Charles C Thomas Co., 301–327 E. Laurence Ave., Springfield, IL 62705.
>
> *Exploring Inner Space: Awareness Games for All Ages,* by Hills and Rozman; University of the Trees Press, P.O. Box 644, Boulder Creek, CA 95006.
>
> *Educating the Forgotten Half,* by Lee and Pulvino; Kendal Hunt, 2460 Kerper Ave., Dubuque, IA 52001.

The Complexity of the Thought Process

In 1926, Graham Wallas proposed a four-step thinking process:[26]

1. Preparation. (This is the reception of data and is exemplified by in-class time.)
2. Incubation. (A solitary period to let it all sink in.) Incubation is often lacking in a "normal" school day.
3. Illumination. (Eureka!) Given a chance at incubation, the right hemisphere comes through for you.
4. Verification. (Either by reassurance from others or practical application.) Often the GC doesn't need external verification (grades and assorted rewards) because self-knowledge can be enough. An interesting note here: Many parents claim to prefer intrinsic motivation and the joy of learning for their children (internal verification), in reality demanding high grades, scholarships and awards (external verification).

J. P. Guilford theorized that the intellect is made up of at least 120 separate factors that present themselves as elements of cognition, memory, convergent thinking, divergent thinking and evaluation. He organized these factors (some of which have yet to be defined) into a cubelike model known as the Structure of the Intellect (SOI). Each factor was thus characterized according to (1) operation, (2) content and (3) products of thought.[27]

He further suggested that intellect could be taught. Divergent thinking, for example (the skill most often overlooked in "normal" educational programs) is taught through exercises that resemble party games, brainstorming, etc. "How many uses can you list for a brick?" "How many words can you make out of the word 'valentine'?"

The Peabody Language Development Kits (and other popular market games) try to enhance divergent thinking with "I wonder" cards. The child is shown a scene and asked, "I wonder what will happen next?" And in California, Dr. Mary Meeker has evolved a series of teachers' guides and workbooks that fulfill the requirements of an Individual Education Plan (IEP).[28] (The requirements of an IEP are that it diagnose need and list specific instructional and behavioral goals, and it is required for most federal and state money; also see above, p. 135n.)

Actually, every child should be taught this way. Just about every school principal will tell you that her teachers do just that. However, the important point for parents to remember is that your child will stand a far greater chance of receiving an IEP if teachers are required to (1) compose and commit such a plan to paper, (2) seek your advice as to your child's special needs and (3) show you evidence of real progress and achievement. ("Don't just tell me he's doing fine in school. Show me some examples of what he has learned.") I feel very strongly about this point. As parents, we get only what we demand.

Assorted Methods, Ramifications and Interpretations

Mentorship. Because GCs often identify with older children and/or adults, the tutorial or mentor approach to education has proven to be a highly effective system. Mentors may be practitioners of a skill, artisans or other knowledgeable individuals who come into the classroom for demonstration and leadership. A mentor may also be a partner in a study group.

Apprenticeships and internships. Using the same principles as the mentorship, many specialists in gifted education advocate early ventures into the "real world."

Token economy. In the token economy, the classroom is run like an economic community. Students are given tokens (points, poker chips, etc.) as rewards for goods and services. (Tokens can be exchanged for class privileges, candy or other "treats.") Economic cycles are studied by establishing management systems, industry, government and social services in a giant community role play.

School credit for community involvement. (An example is Philadelphia's Parkway Program.) In these programs, art is taught in the museums, social studies in social agencies, commerce in business, etc. Students also receive credit for volunteer work in hospitals, schools, churches, etc.

Magnet schools for GCs of a geographic area. This would include schools such as the High School of Music and Art and the Bronx High School of Science (a program boasting two recent Nobel Prizewinners in physics), both in New York City.

Return to the classics. There has been a reemergence of classical studies for GCs. These include philosophy for third- and fourth-graders and seventh-grade classes in leadership and the law. A public school in Plainfield, N.J., conducts logic classes for gifted fifth-graders.

Return to foreign languages. A return to Latin, Greek and Hebrew is particularly notable among increased study of foreign languages.

Independent studies. An example is the program administered by the Hamden-New Haven (Conn.) Cooperative Education Center.

Futuristics. The proponents of futuristics see current educational systems as primitive and unsophisticated. They contend that in a world of incredible technology and expanding data, schools continue to dwell upon the details of past events.

In addition, the argument goes, they do so with antiquated teaching methods. Why, they ask, should a student be taught in only one traditional model: in a classroom, at one specific hour of a specific day, with the books, chalkboards, lectures and examinations of centuries past? But it is the actual thinking processes being used in these schools that most disturb the futurists. Schools often teach that there is one correct answer and students must converge upon that single point. This, they feel, leads to the perpetuation of misinformation and outdated trivia. More importantly, the student observes that in the world outside of the classroom, issues may have several valid solutions or points of view.

As an alternative, they suggest teaching open-ended anticipation of the logical causes and effects of real-life problems (divergent thinking about the future). This is most often accomplished through:

1. Scenario writing. Students take a particular trend (e.g., water pollution) into the future, analyzing both the negative and positive paths it could take. In the negative scenario, for example, one factor such as technology could result in overindustrialization, chemical accidents and an eventual poisoning of the planet's water supply. The positive scenario could find that technology (e.g., desalinization, improved filtration or the creation of artificial water) could solve the problem.

2. Creative problem-solving. Real-life problems are often ill-defined. In this technique, the student must explore and define aspects of the problem before progressing to alternative solutions.

3. The Cross Impact Matrix. This graphic representation is used to stimulate discussion and exploration of cause and effect relationships.

	Population	Technology	Politics
Population			
Technology			
Politics			

For example: What negative and positive effects would either increased or decreased technology have on population and politics (politics as related to population and technology, etc.)?
4. Global futures. This process is a careful analysis of the future events of the world as determined by both the positive and negative aspects of developing trends. These trends would include economics, technology, politics, religions, geological events, etc.

For information about including futuristics in existing curricula, write:

The World Future Society
4916 Saint Elmo Ave.
Washington, DC 20014

Dr. Charles Whaley
Burris Laboratory School
Ball State University
Muncie, IN 47306

Futuristics seems difficult and too abstract at first. But you go through much the same processes when you make decisions such as where to send your child to school, your own career directions or how to feed and entertain visiting relatives.

Gifted education in specific subject areas. In "Education of Children with High Mental Ability," James Dunlap presents the following suggestions for gifted education:

Math: going beyond computation to the mastery of theory.
Science: (1) stressing conceptualization, reflection and analysis; (2) teaching scientific principles by having students discover them with tools that were historically accurate for the discovering scientists.
Social Studies: (1) more discussion and emphasis upon human motivation and emotions during historic events; (2) dramatization of historic events to stress the responsibilities of leadership and the significance of ethics.
Language arts: allowing for more creative expression.[29]

Meanwhile, there are several current trends in public education that can have *negative* impact upon GCs. Joyce Van Tassel, consultant and national president, the Association for the Gifted, has identified three critical concerns for the parents of GCs.[30]

Minimum Competency Testing. "We are for maximum competency," she says. This tendency to stress minimum levels of accomplishment leads to expectation levels that are too low for GCs. Van Tassel continues, "Instead of meeting a pre-determined standard, we are for taking off the ceiling around the notion of how high a child should achieve."

Back-to-basics. In the school stressing a "back-to-basics" philosophy, the classroom teacher too often interprets this as being only the three Rs. Therefore, those areas that should be basic to the GC are never covered: study skills, coping skills, problem solving, creativity, etc. GCs can and should be exempt from basics at which they demonstrate proficiency.

Mainstreaming. Mainstreaming is the deemphasizing of separate classes for special learning needs. Born out of a search for the appropriate placement of handicapped children (P.L. 94-142 calls for education that is "the least restrictive and thus closer to normal school environment"), mainstreaming does not philosophically or functionally help the GC reach his greatest potential.

Mainstreaming is an example of the philosophical flip-flopping so often seen in educational practice. About thirty years ago many educators felt that handicapped students were sinking in the academic mainstream. Special ability grouping seemed the answer. After about twenty years of such grouping, after research verifying the advantages of "special education" teachers, after incredible advancements in the education of these "exceptional students," after all this success, someone came up with the idea of trying—you guessed it—mainstreaming. Although certainly a goal for many handicapped students, the premature reintroduction of some back into the mainstream from which they had been so mercifully pulled seemed beyond belief. When it happened I was a counselor in a large high school. One mentally retarded student became so terrified of entering the mainstream that she literally lost herself for three weeks. Every day she would go to her homeroom for attendance check, mingle in the halls as classes changed and hide in the bathrooms while classes were in session. She remembered her experiences with normal children as frustrating, humiliating and negative. She saw no reason to return to this old system. A lot of special education teachers and counselors would agree with her.

The rationale behind mainstreaming handicapped children is a critical concern for the parents of GCs. Many educators feel that GCs, like the handicapped, have social and intellectual interests and abilities that separate them from their chronological peers. They reason that mainstreaming will lessen this separation. It could be called the "throw 'em in the pot and let 'em mingle" theory. The handicapped will learn from the normal and vice versa. The gifted will learn from the normal and vice versa. Everyone will be more normal because of the experience.

Two types of advancement are at issue: social and academic. Mainstreaming *may* mean social and/or academic advancement for some handicapped students. (It meant neither for the student discussed earlier.) Mainstreaming *may* mean social advancement for the GC—particularly if the GC in question has difficulty relating to chronological peers. Mainstreaming most certainly *does not* mean academic advancement for any GC. Rather, it means academic suppression.

Remember: 1. Mainstreaming is an educational trend. It can come or go, and 2. Mainstreaming does not promote academic advancement for GC. You as a parent must decide whether or not your child should risk academic suppression for the possibility of social advancement.

WHO GETS IN? WHO STAYS OUT?

This matter of identification seems to be the real stumbling block for the full-fledged acceptance of gifted education. It's a bit like the controversy over capital punishment. Many people will agree to the execution of a psychopath who willfully and brutally murders innocents. Others maintain that no one should ever be executed lest someone be killed in error. There is a vast middle ground of controversy.

Many people will agree that children with superior levels of genius require special challenge. Others maintain that no one should ever be singled out lest someone be omitted in error. There is a vast middle ground of controversy.

While one can argue that the psychopath can be restrained and not killed, the GC without special education cannot be held in such suspended animation. Atrophy, maladjustment of personality, talents never fulfilled, missed opportunities and lessons never learned are, in large measure, irreparable.

The identification of participants in gifted education is usually a community-determined blending of the following:

1. IQ test scores—group
2. IQ test scores—individual
3. School records
4. Teacher judgments
5. Parent interviews
6. Applicant interviews

E. Paul Torrance has suggested that the following criteria may be more valid for those GCs with skills in creativity, leadership and the performing or visual arts:

1. Observations of behavior, especially creativity
2. Observations of children in environments other than schools
3. Observations of children in situations requiring gifted behavior:

   • Exercises in which child expresses feelings
   • Exercises in which child does planning
   • Exercises in which child is challenged to defend negative ideas to peers
   • Exercises in which child is encouraged to discuss complex, seemingly hopeless problems and still be creative
   • Exercises in which child is asked to do a previously accomplished task, but in a new way (improvisation)[31]

New Trends in Identification

Off-level testing: Research at Johns Hopkins University has shown us that traditional achievement tests given to "appropriate" age and grade level GCs merely group those GCs in the 90–95th percentile range. This information is totally ineffectual for program planning and individual development since it in no way diagnoses the real abilities and needs of each child. However, when a seventh-grade GC is given a test scaled for college freshmen, the ceiling is literally taken off. A score on such a test would give a more accurate representation of where the child is actually functioning.[32]

More reliance upon aptitude tests. The researchers at Johns Hopkins also determined that the IQ score was totally irrelevant when assessing superior ability in specific areas.[33]

Preschool screening. As is true with handicapped students, early identification of giftedness can prevent the underachievement problems so often seen in school-age children.[34]

Concerted efforts to identify subpopulations. There are a few isolated programs that strive to identify specific GCs with "low visibility." These would include culturally disadvantaged GCs and handicapped GCs.[35]

Research into the identification of underachieving gifted females: As you can well imagine, the question of whether or not gifted males and gifted females are significantly different is far from resolved.

In "Is the Gifted Girl an Anomaly?" Carolyn Callahan, professor at the University of Virginia, raises some heretofore unanswered questions:

1. Are females taught to fear success?
2. Are females really in control of their lives and achievements?
3. Have females been taught to be satisfied with less achievement?
4. Do females fail to learn the visual/spatial relationships so essential for math and other quantitative skills be-

cause social inhibitions regarding play lead to retarded gross-motor development? ("Sally, honey, don't climb that tree; you'll tear your good dress.")

5. Do elementary and high school literature assignments stress stories with male role models on the assumption that it is more difficult to hold the boys' attention? (After all, girls willingly read anything; but boys won't read stories about girls.)

6. In preschool experiences, are females still encouraged to play house while the males play ball?

Callahan also reports that many studies of high-achieving adult women indicate they have "greater self-confidence, more ego strength, greater rebellious independence and a greater rejection of outside influence."

She suggests that educators provide the following for the female GC:

1. Visual/spatial activities.
2. Positive female role models engaging in problem-solving situations.
3. Opportunities for interaction with successful female GCs and adults (mentors).
4. Opportunities to establish personal goals.
5. Counseling for females GCs who meet family resistance.[36]

And so, when it comes to identification, the scholars debate and the school boards argue over ways to avoid the misdiagnosis of one suspected GC. Meanwhile, the so-called "verified" or "obviously" gifted linger on waiting lists for the few existing programs in gifted education.

Conversely, we do not have the ability to predict those skills that can cause a "bright," "high-average," "academically talented," but not "technically gifted" student to plug away to superior achievement. Shouldn't success, after all, be some kind of giftedness too?

Dr. John Feldhusen is vehement about this position. His Super Saturday enrichment program is open to students generally considered "nongifted" (115–120 IQ range) but who exhibit superior organizational skills and/or high levels of motivation. In a recent interview for the Indiana Association for the Gifted, he expressed concern over the tendency of some schools to select participants in gifted education solely on the basis of specific IQ or achievement test scores. When there is any doubt, he continues, "A child should be permitted to try out." Then, if performance does not follow expectation, the child should be excluded for the overall success of the program.[37] It is perhaps this chilling possibility that frightens the parents and educators of "borderline" cases.

I believe this is an unresolvable dilemma as long as we think of gifted education as chocolate drops to be passed out only to the brightest and most talented. "Chocolate-drop-education" demands that we make decisions we seem to be unable and/or unwilling to pursue.

The proponents of gifted education agree on several overall points:

GCs should be taught research and information retrieval skills.

The education of the GC should foster habits of logical thinking.

Every attempt must be made to expand the opportunities for inquiry and creative output.

Our society can no longer afford to force these children through inappropriate and inadequate school experience.

Robert Kirschenbaum, a former teacher of the gifted and a consultant to emerging programs, has said that teaching our GCs to play games and solve puzzles isn't nearly enough. Rather than thinking of them as potential leaders of tomorrow, we must think of them as leaders of today. Gifted education must put students in the role of "changing agents—striving to have an impact on the reality of the present. [They] must become familiar with . . . producing change or resolving a real concern in the community."[38]

LET'S TALK ABOUT THE POWER STRUCTURE
Teachers

Teachers are like peanuts in the shell: you can't tell much from the outside, but a good one leaves you wanting more, and a rotten one leaves a nasty taste in your mouth. It's easy to pick on them. Some teachers have the functional intelligence of a broken doorknob. With a little persuasion, they turn to the left and they turn to the right. Occasionally, they even open the door.

It is indisputable that myopic educators can seriously damage a GC. It is indisputable that a teacher who doesn't understand, objects to or doesn't believe in gifted education can sabotage the best-laid plans of a state curriculum consultant, a willing school board or an enlightened principal.

I could even give personal evidence: Mrs. Grimm, who flunked my fourth-grade poem because it "sounded too good to have been written by a kid." Mrs. Wilder, who punished my classroom prattle by painting my tongue with Mercurochrome.

Nothing, not the educational philosophy, not the physical facility, not the fun you have at parents' meetings, can take the place of a sincere, educated individual who cares about your child. The teacher is and always has been *everything*.

The comments of a gifted student say it all: "When you're wandering ... through elementary school ... vaguely aware you're different in a superior sense and able to read ... before you even entered school, you may not have much sense of direction." The writer continues, "What can be invaluable is someone taking an interest in your case and telling you about the potential of extraordinary capabilities you may not know you have."[39]

Still another GC tells us, "Starting with the second grade and on through high school, there have been nine teachers I've admired. I admired them because their own strength and natural rapport with students in turn demanded our respect. Kindness, sensitivity and intelligence were among their many qualities and virtues. Most importantly, they made each student feel significant, as if each one of us had a part ... in reserve."[40]

According to statistics, teachers seem to be poor judges as to who is gifted. In *Behavior of Exceptional Children, An Introduction,* James Payne cites several studies in which this has been shown to be true. In one, 31 percent of the children labeled gifted by their teachers were not found to be gifted by a panel of unbiased educators. More importantly, 55 percent of those students determined to be gifted by the panel had not been selected by their teachers.[41]

The evidence seems clear that teachers can overlook GCs who are underachievers, nonmotivated or behavioral problems. ("Go away, kid, you bother me.")

I can close my eyes and see how these kids are not selected. Teacher: "Jerome, since you can't seem to finish your history assignment without disturbing your neighbors, you can take these papers down to the office, sit up here by my desk, or work on something a little easier."

In more than twenty years of being a student, I have had more good teachers than bad. And even in his relatively short school career, our GC has been truly gifted with several inspired and inspiring teachers.

Gifted Teachers

Simply put, gifted teachers are those teachers who:

Understand themselves.

Know the traits and behaviors of GCs.

Have concern for the process of learning as well as with the product of learning. (God bless my Algebra II teacher. He used to give us partial credit for a problem that had been logically solved, but blown by a careless error in addition.)

Provide alternative learning strategies.

Give feedback rather than judgment.

Are open to and even supportive of creative and cognitive risk taking.[42]

Teachers judged successful by high-achieving, gifted students in Georgia:

Expressed high achievement needs.
Were considered to be gifted themselves.
Were more student-oriented.
Were judged more stimulating and imaginative in class-
room techniques.[43]

And in the article "Creative Teaching Makes a Difference,"
E. Paul Torrance defines teachers who were successful with
GCs as those who:

Allowed them to work alone and at their own pace.
Were receptive and active listeners.
Were not afraid to try new methods and improvisations.[44]

Nevertheless, when it comes to finding a gifted teacher for
your GC, you have to become particularly skillful at ferreting
out friend from foe.
Some guidelines:
Plan your approach. Think through the basic educational alternatives. Decide which appeals to you and which you think
would be best for your GC. Involve your GC in this decision as
soon as possible.
Encourage a dialogue. If the teacher understands your expectations, hesitancies and/or commitments and if you understand
the reasons why they can or cannot be met, you're on your way
toward building a working relationship. If you really feel that
your four-year-old should be taught to read, then say so. Be
prepared to listen if the teacher has other ideas. And be prepared to find another teacher or even another school if you
can't work it out.
I believe that sometimes a teacher can communicate mar-
velously with children and still be quite uncomfortable and
thus ineffectual when talking to parents. Nevertheless, be sus-
picious of a teacher who always talks to you as if you were "sitting in the little desk."
Act as if you have some manners yourself. Use a little common
sense. Don't go charging up to the classroom teacher with
something like: "We just found out that Arnold is an under-
achieving genius. What are you going to do about it?" What can

you expect? (I know what I'd say to you, and you wouldn't like it.)

Don't be outmaneuvered by jargon. Ask questions when you don't understand. Too many parents come away from a conversation with the teacher having no idea of what was said. If you've never heard the term "culminating experiential activity," ask what it means. If a teacher says that your child needs to develop "more of a self-environmental relationship," don't be embarrassed to say you don't understand. (I'll give you a hint, lots of teachers don't either.)

Ask the teacher to explain the educational objectives behind an activity. At one school our GC attended, several parents were disgruntled over what appeared to be an inordinate amount of each day spent discussing the weather. The teachers had so skillfully hidden the lesson plan that it was hard to see that talk about the sunny day was an interweaving of physical science; conceptualizing abstractions (calendars and clocks); mathematics ("How many sunny days have we had this month?"); fine motor and association skills ("Put the picture of the sun and the number for the day on the calendar board"); language arts and public speaking skills ("Can you give us a sentence that tells us what kind of day it is today?") and of course, the ever-present socialization skills ("Elaine, it's Alan's turn to count the sunny days").

Take qualifications with a grain of salt. Education is a field where a lot can be learned through hand-to-hand combat in the trenches. A teacher with limited experiences in "formal" gifted education programs can still be a sensitive, scholarly mentor. Conversely, matriculation through some university programs in education merely requires: (1) the payment of tuition, (2) good note-taking/regurgitation skills and (3) a tenacious rearend (for sitting through all those dreary educational theory courses).

Talk to your GC. Talk particularly about what goes on when the classroom door closes. You have to be creatively covert here since if you ask, "What did you do in school today?" you're likely to get "Nothing" for an answer.

Also talk to your GC about those times when he must realistically adapt to even the most bland educational experience: "I'm sorry—we can't change things; we can't move; we can't afford Our Town's Country Day. You'll just have to get interested in the Scouts."

Don't be satisfied with an annual checkup. Parents' Night and Open House are terrific concepts, but if that's the only time you ever talk to the teacher, your GC could be in serious trouble. Obviously you can't be running up to the school every day, but you must maintain the dialogue if you're to understand your GC and your role in her development.

Be particularly alert to the teacher who doesn't seem to have time for a conference, or who can say nothing more specific than, "Jamie's such a sweet girl; she's doing fine."

Don't leave loose ends. Restate any bargains and ask for a resolution date: "Well, then, we've agreed to watch the math progress carefully for one month. I'll make certain he does his homework *before* soccer practice."

Follow up. "I've been looking at this math business very carefully now and . . ."

Principals

Remember that memory aid to differentiate "principal" from "principle"? "The principal is your 'pal.' " Well, sometimes yes, and sometimes no. There are those who run their schools as would a feudal lord, but most principals are pulled one way by their teachers, pulled one way by the school board, pulled one way by the superintendent, pulled one way by parents and pulled another way by the cafeteria workers' union. This is the person who hears every complaint from what they're smoking in the bathrooms to how much it costs to have a roof repaired.

It's the principal who has to tell the sixty-year-old librarian she can't paste paper dresses on the bra ads in *Seventeen*. It's the principal who has to settle the arguments in the English department's Textbook Review Committee. It's the principal who has to balance the budget and still have enough for some good coffee in the teacher's lounge. In an article, "Probing the Pressures on Principals," William Wayson reflects, "The literature on the principalship makes me wonder why anyone would want to take on the job."[45]

But the factor that gives them the most heartache should give us parents some pause. In a 1977 survey of 2000 public secondary school principals throughout the country, the National Institute of Education cited their most serious problem as "parental lack of interest in their children's progress and their lack of involvement with the school. . . ." This conclusion was similar to one drawn in a study by the National Association of Secondary School Principals.[46]

I feel we parents should seriously consider this charge. Ask yourself if you spend as much time reviewing your child's educational progress as you do:

Comparison shopping for a stereo.
Clipping cereal coupons.
Matching her socks to her school dresses.

We have no one to blame but ourselves if our GCs wallow in nonproductive, even detrimental, school experiences.

Superintendents and Assorted Subordinates

The Superintendent's office houses the administrative professionals of any school system. In some communities, they are as remote as the bureaucrats in the Office of Mucilage and Mimeograph Fluid, and they may or may not make the buses run on time. In other communities, they are the power behind the throne.

School Boards: The Throne

You can write to your superintendent, you can scream at your principal, you can sob on your teacher's shoulder, but Sandpile 101 is a concept spawned at a school board meeting.

The purpose of a school board is to interpret to the professional educators the wants, needs, expectations and demands of the community. (The operant word here is "interpret.") The school board is therefore a visible scapegoat when things go wrong.

"In the first place, God made idiots; this was for practice; then He made school boards," said Mark Twain,[47] expressing what must have been a common belief in his day.

The culpability of school board members is short-lived, however, because we elect them. And how many voters approach the school board ballot armed only with the skill to discern "apparently male" from "apparently female" names?

The public schools must provide for the needs of all children; and that includes the gifted. In addition, it is the responsibility of the community to make the school board aware of those needs. That includes the segment of the community whose children will benefit most from such programs, the parents of GCs. All the rules of persuasion, diplomacy, politics and street fighting go into play at this point. I have seen a situation where frustrated parents of frustrated GCs so alienated a school board that they were run out of a meeting on the figurative rail. Even after continued volunteer service to the school and a marshalling of other parents, no appreciable move toward gifted education was ever made by school board members. In a neighboring community, similar tactics resulted in a three-year pilot program (federally funded) and resounding "hurrahs" from everyone who formerly doubted and then suddenly "knew it was a great idea all along."

THE LARGER PROBLEM

I've opened the cannons upon both public and private schools. And while I won't take any of it back, I should try to give some balance. For the most part, gifted education isn't working because, for the most part, education isn't working. (And by now, you know I'm going to tell you why I think so.)

1. The schools are asked to assume too many of the responsibilities of parenting.

2. In too many cases, it's no fun being a teacher anymore. (And it isn't just the money.)

The public school I attended was parochial, unsophisticated

and we had to use the gym for an auditorium. But I could always count on one thing: the day I didn't do my homework or the day I pulled a stunt was likely to be the day my mother brought in the costumes for the class play or the day my dad and the principal both stopped off for a beer at the American Legion. The school was more than just a place to go each day; and the things I did in school (right and wrong) came home with me.

As parents, it is our fault that the schools are failing. We have dumped virtually every aspect of child rearing right at the school's steps, and it was never intended to take on such a role.

I heard a former teacher explain her "final straw." She had received a parent's note that read, "I told my kid he doesn't have to do what you say anymore."

I was once summoned to the principal's office accused of calling one of my students a "liar." What I had actually said, "Have you really thought through that statement?" never seemed to enter the discussion. The fact that the kid was indeed a liar never entered the discussion either. Rather than working on a plan to help this student recognize and reach a learning goal (not lying), the parent and the principal agreed that I wouldn't call him a liar again.

Ultimately this brings us to the status of the classroom teacher. I did suffer through the fifth grade with Mrs. Wilder (I've already told you about her; but she had this other trick of putting a rubber band on your wrist, tying a knot and snapping it on the soft underside, near those big veins from your hand), yet I could look forward to the sixth grade with Mrs. Woolsey.

Mrs. Woolsey, Mr. Hopkins, Mrs. Hale, Dr. White—I can actually name the people who made some difference in my life. Is the difference in education now just that "they don't make 'em like they used to"? Is it that schools of education have become hamburger factories, stamping out teachers like Mac-Burgers? Don't people want education anymore?

Even the most accurate finger pointing will do little to help at this stage. Strategies for radical activism are the focus of the following chapter about P.O.P.s (Powerfully Organized Parents).

Notes

1. Ivan Illich, *Deschooling Society,* Harper & Row, New York, 1972.
2. Roland Barth, *Open Education and the American School,* Agathon Press, New York, 1972.
3. Lena Gitter, *The Montessori Way,* Special Child Publications, Seattle, 1970.
4. James M. Dunlap, "The Education of Children with High Mental Ability," in *Education of Exceptional Children and Youth,* 3d ed., ed. William Crickshank and G. Orville Johnson, Prentice-Hall, Englewood Cliffs, N.J., 1975.
5. John C. Gowan in a speech to the Central Indiana Association for Gifted Children, Indianapolis, Oct. 25, 1979.
6. Joseph L. French, "The Highly Intelligent Drop-Out," *Psychology and Education of the Gifted,* 2nd ed., ed. Barbe and Renzulli, Irvington Publishers, New York, 1975.
7. Dunlap, op. cit.
8. Leta S. Hollingworth, "An Enrichment Curriculum for Rapid Learners at Public School 500 Speyer School," *Teachers College Record,* 39:4, 1938.
9. Sidney P. Marland, "Send Up More Sputnicks," *Gifted Child Quarterly,* 17:3, Autumn 1978.
10. Gill Caudill in a speech to the Noblesville Association for the Gifted, Feb. 13, 1980, Forest Hill Elementary School, Noblesville, Ind.
11. Clinkenbeard-Fisher Report, "State Services for Gifted and Talented," Office of Gifted and Talented, Washington, D.C., 1979.
12. Harold Lyon, "Talent Down the Drain," *American Education,* 8:12, October 1972.
13. Clinkenbeard-Fisher Report.
14. Joseph S. Renzulli, "Enrichment Triad Model: A Guide for Developing Defensible Programs for the Gifted and Talented," Part I, *The Gifted Child Quarterly,* 20:30, Fall 1976.
15. John F. Feldhusen and Margaret B. Kolloff, "A Three-Stage Model for Gifted Education," *Gifted/Creative/Talented Children,* No. 4, September–October 1978.
16. Jack W. Birch, "Early School Admission for Mentally Advanced Children," *Exceptional Children,* 21:3, December 1954.
17. *On Being Gifted,* written by participants in the National Student Symposium on the Education of the Gifted and Talented, Mark Krueger, Project Director. Sponsored by the American Association for Gifted Children. Walker & Co., New York, 1978.
18. Julian C. Stanley and William C. George, "SMPY's Ever-Increasing P_4," *Gifted Child Quarterly,* 24:1, Winter 1980.

19. Michael Wallach, "Care and Feeding of the Gifted," *Contemporary Psychology,* 23:9, 1978.
20. John Feldhusen and Ann Wyman, "Super Saturday: Design & Implementation of Purdue's Special Program for Gifted Education," *Gifted Child Quarterly,* forthcoming.
21. N. Hobbs, "Motivation to High Achievement," in *Working with Superior Students. Theories and Practices,* ed. B. Shertzer, Science Research Associates, Chicago, 1960.
22. Rudolf Flesch, ed., *The New Book of Unusual Quotations,* Harper & Row, New York, 1966.
23. *McGraw-Hill Encyclopedia of World Biography,* vol. 10, McGraw-Hill, New York, 1973.
24. *Who's Who in America,* 40th ed., 1978–79, vol. 1.
25. Everett McKinley Dirksen and Herbert Prochnow, eds., *Quotation Finder,* Harper & Row, New York, 1971.
26. Graham Wallas, *The Art of Thought,* C. A. Watts, Inc., London, 1926.
27. J. P. Guilford, "Three Faces of Intellect," *American Psychologist,* vol. 14, 1959.
28. Mary N. Meeker, *Learning to Plan, Judge and Make Decisions: A Structure of Intellect Evaluation Workbook,* SOI Institute, El Segundo, Calif., 1976.
29. Dunlap, op. cit.
30. Joyce Van Tassel, "National Interests and Concerns in Gifted Education," speech before the Indiana Federation Council for Exceptional Children, Feb. 29, 1980, Indianapolis.
31. E. Paul Torrance, *Gifted Children in the Classroom,* The Psychological Foundations of Education Series, Macmillan, New York, 1965.
32. Van Tassel, op. cit.
33. John Stanley, ed., *The Gifted and the Creative: A Fifty-Year Perspective,* Johns Hopkins University Press, Baltimore, 1977.
34. Van Tassel, op. cit.
35. Ibid.
36. Carolyn Callahan, "Is the Gifted Girl an Anomaly?" *Roeper Review II,* February–March 1980.
37. Amy Cox and Ruth Pickard, eds., "Spotlight on People, Dr. John Feldhusen," Newsletter of the Indiana Association for the Gifted, 2:2, Fall 1979.
38. Robert Kirschenbaum, "Who Are the Gifted and Why Are They Different?" *Roeper Review II,* September 1979.
39. *On Being Gifted.*
40. *On Being Gifted.*
41. James Payne, "The Gifted," *Behavior of Exceptional Children: An Introduction to Special Education,* ed. Norris G. Haring, Merrill, Columbus, Ohio, 1974.
42. Joan B. Nelson and Donald L. Cleland, "The Role of the Teacher of Gifted and Creative Children," an article in *Reading for the*

Gifted and Creative Student, ed. Paul A. Witty, International Reading Association, Newark, Del., 1971.

43. William E. Bishop, "Characteristics of Teachers Judged Successful by Intellectually Gifted High Achieving High School Students," unpublished doctoral disseration, Indiana Central College, Indianapolis.

44. E. Paul Torrance, "Creative Teaching Makes a Difference," *Creativity: Its Educational Implication,* ed. Gowen, Demos, and Torrance, Wiley, New York, 1967.

45. William W. Wayson, "Probing the Pressures on Principals," *The National Elementary Principal,* vol. 58, March 1979.

46. Susan Abramowitz and Ellen Tenenbaum, "High School '77: A Survey of Public Secondary School Principals," National Institute of Education, HEW, Washington, D.C., December 1978.

47. Flesch, op. cit.

5

Parent Groups—
Strength in Numbers

Okay, you've read the book. You know a little more about GCs.
You were right: your kid is one. Now what? If you live in a community that has already begun to address the special learning
needs of your child, your action may be as uncomplicated as
contacting the appropriate school, arranging for an interview
and getting the kid to take a bath.

What if you live in Bean Blossom, U.S.A.? What if you have
overheard the superintendent of schools say, "We don't need
any neurotic geniuses in our schools. All we want is to turn out
some good, old-fashioned, normal American kids"? What if
your school's principal laughs and says, "Look, everybody
thinks their kids are gifted"?

It's time for my famous second-grade story. Friends have
heard it a thousand times because I use it as a parable for all
seasons. We each have a few "meaningful events" that shape
our attitudes and beliefs. One of mine happened in the corridor
of Dexter Elementary, Evansville, Indiana. Classes were
changing, and as a naïve first-grader I was overwhelmed by the
clamor of the older kids going upstairs to the "big grades." A

neighborhood friend appeared and must have asked how things were going, because I said that school was really getting hard.

"Hard," he scoffed. "You think it's hard now—wait 'til you get to the second grade. They expect us to write words that aren't even on the board!"

"Christ!" I thought (though probably not in that language). "Write words that aren't even on the board! I'll never make it through that!"

Confucius may have said it better with his long journey/first step story; but my version makes the same point. Every time I am frustrated by an overwhelming task, I remember how I eventually learned to write words that weren't even on the board.

You will be able to guarantee challenging, stimulating and enriching educational experiences for your GC if you will just stop worrying about it and get it done. Or as my Germanic mother-in-law says to inspire the troops, "Off your seat and on your feet!"

One answer may be to join or organize a group of GC parents. Notice the crucial verb form. You must examine yourself and your school community before you make such a choice. In the first place, not everybody is a joiner. I've met many GC parents who look upon the idea of joining arms in parental coalition as something between a union solidarity march and a sorority candlelight. Both may be good for the spirit, but the real long-term gains are nebulous.

It is possible for a group of Powerfully Organized Parents (P.O.P.s) to exert an incredibly positive impact upon an entire educational system.

A case in point: Five suburban Minneapolis school boards were encouraged into a cooperative enrichment program for the area's GCs. The West Suburban Consortium for Gifted and Talented Youth obtained private foundation grants and state summer school money. The result was a summer program for 400 GCs, who were able to work in Latin, journalism, acting, geology and college survival skills.[1] And another: The Washington Township School District of Indianapolis was encouraged (through the vocal and spirited demands of P.O.P.s) to apply for federal funding for gifted education. The result was a pilot program now loved and praised by all.

P.O.P.s can also cause a bitter, disruptive gang war something akin to in-laws fighting over the patriarchal estate. I will admit to having had my doubts when I've attended such gatherings. But then, I didn't like Weight Watchers either.

Let's look at it a bit more closely.

The Fun Part of Grouping

Banding together can provide a strong, vocal voice loud enough to wake up the school board. It is a fact: Group concerns usually have precedence over individual ones. Parents coming out of isolation can:

- lend support in the day-to-day frustration of rearing a GC. ("I don't understand it. If he's so smart, why can't he learn to use toilet paper?")
- provide opportunities to share experiences. ("You know, I couldn't tell my neighbors, but in her spare time, Janice is building a Fortran computer system.")
- help to put problems in perspective. ("What a relief! I thought I had the only six-year-old who scolded me for not alphabetizing the canned goods.")

Organized parents also provide socialization networks that allow GCs to relate to their peers. Through the special school our son attends, he's met and developed friendships with GCs 40 to 60 miles from our home. Yes, yes, everybody does have to learn to live with everyone else—but it's nice to have some friends it's especially easy to be with.

Often the parents of GCs are interesting, stimulating adults of very diverse backgrounds. It's fun to know them. More importantly for the kids, they can form a reference/resource pool for all kinds of activities. One of the dads builds a caterpillar cage in anticipation of metamorphosis; a mother organizes a conversational Russian class; a grandmother teaches the kids how to repair their toys; a grandpa shows them how to "grow their own" (vegetables, that is)—suddenly you have the nucleus for a dandy little enrichment program.

What's Not So Fun
About a Parent Group

First and foremost, you stand to make a lot of enemies. If you think the people who first advocated no-smoking zones in restaurants had it rough, wait until you hit a community with a group of parents who think their kids are "gifted, talented, intelligent, genius, very smart or all of the above." Do not expect applause from the PTA.

You run the risk of alienating the professional educators if you sharply threaten their perimeters. I'm not saying they don't deserve a few jabs, but let's talk about real life for a minute.

If you are an adult, aged twenty-five to, say, forty, and have not spent a full day in an elementary school classroom since you graduated to junior high, you may be (to put it politely) "out of touch." Chances are that what you learned in the fifth grade is now being taught to second graders. And what you learned in the first grade is common knowledge in the preschools. Those educators who are conscientious have been hustling just to keep pace with the overwhelming explosion of facts and data that have become available to today's children.

"In fourteen-and-ninety-two, Columbus sailed the ocean blue." Well, yes he did, but he certainly did not discover America—not as we were taught twenty-five years ago. The Vikings hit Canada; the Indians traipsed down through Alaska; the Polynesians probably made it to Central America and the Druids talked about coming, but couldn't get organized. Everybody but Howard Johnson was here before Columbus. And one logistical problem of modern school life is that it takes more time and greater creativity to cover new theories, information and discoveries. Simply stating facts and dates is passé. The teacher must examine the psychological, economic, sociological, philosophical, cultural and experiential motivations of historic events.

The evolution in social studies is mild when compared to that of science. When I took high school chemistry, there were only 101 elements on the periodic table. We did physics experiments that were not much more advanced than using heat to contract a hard-boiled egg into a glass milk bottle. Biology involved dissecting a bullfrog (I called mine Fred until we got to the reproductive system) and looking at pond water under a 30X microscope.

Times have also been tense for the school administrators. Aside from problems with the curricula and updating equipment, the teachers go out on strike; it's hard as hell to keep bus drivers; it's taken years to get the courts to say they can open the kids' lockers (and you know what's in them); costs are going up and the necklines on the cheerleaders' sweaters are coming down. I wouldn't want the job. Then one bright afternoon, in comes the representative from the Association of Parents of the Gifted and Talented who says her kids aren't getting enough intellectual stimulation.

I'm not saying your group's claims won't be justified, but plan your approach with care. Unless you can afford to keep transferring your kids every time you have it out with the faculty; unless you can afford a live-in tutor; unless you can provide your child with a suitable alternative, you still need the schools and all they can offer.

HOW TO GET
YOUR VERY OWN GROUP

1. Read one of the following books. (Read both if you're an overachiever.)

Parents Unite! (the complete guide for shaking up
    your children's school)
Phillip and Susan Jones
Wyden Books, New York, 1976

Parent Power (a candid handbook for dealing with
    your child's school)
Martin Buskin
Walker & Co., New York, 1975

2. Plan a meeting.

Put an announcement on the community service board of a
   couple of radio/TV stations.
Ask to put notes in the school menu.
Ask your child who else answers all the questions in class.
   Phone their parents and invite them to your meeting.
Invite school administrators, board members, counselors,
   principals, teachers and anybody else who's interested.

3. Arrange for a speaker.

Lots of state departments of education have gifted education consultants.
Allow for a question-and-answer period.

4. Take names and addresses of participants.
5. Solicit support and membership dues.
6. Announce the date, place and purpose of your next
meeting.

A Humble Statement on
How to Run It Right

1. Know your raw materials. P.O.P.s seem to come in four
categories. Each is essential if your group is to accomplish anything.

The Intellectual Stage-Mothers. Do you remember everything you never wanted to be as a parent of a genius? Well, the
Intellectual Stage-Mothers (and Fathers) are just that. It can
appear to an onlooker that these people spend most of their
time telling each other how smart their kids are. At the drop of
a cocktail napkin they can tell you anything you ever wanted to
know about GCs. They call the superintendent by his first
name and they probably went to grammar school with the
chairman of the state legislature's educational appropriations
committee.

Giftedness is the current cause for them. In college, it was
the fight against fighting or the fight for open dorms; and after
their kids graduate, it'll be something else. They usually offend

a lot of people. They are also your classic motivators with fiery speeches about eroding intellects and assaults upon the mind of a child. I personally never trust zealots, but I accept them as a necessary element of change. Besides, nobody says you have to invite them home for dinner.

A subspecies, the Passive-Aggressive Intellectual Stage-Mother is the parent who truly believes that her child should be translating Proust by the fourth grade. She's for stringing up any teacher who can't conjugate in Latin, and she wants to organize a bake sale for a new word processor. Destiny usually takes care of this type because her kids almost always turn out to be anal-retentive.

The Blanket Seekers. These parents really need the group for security's sake. Thoughts of what to do with the GC are overwhelming. Is she really a genius? What can we do about his limitless energies? Can we keep her intellectually stimulated? Oh, woe is me! The Blanket Seekers naturally flock to the Intellectual Stage-Mothers and the resulting symbiotic relationship can take care of itself in a most benign fashion. They also make excellent telephone committee members.

The Innocent Bystanders. Although often accused of not contributing enough to the cause, I personally think the Innocent Bystanders are a vital component of any activist group. The powers that run the schools look to them as a note of sanity. A certain percentage of calm, stable, nonantagonistic, real-life parents can give you credibility as a policy-provoking body. Even if they just stand around looking parental, you need them if you're to be taken seriously.

The Worker Ants. Finally, to the core of your group. Without Worker Ants, you might as well forget it. These parents provide support, aid and comfort to your GC's school. They volunteer to take the sixth grade on a field trip to study pond life; loan the school the slides of the inside of the Taj Mahal; quietly purchase a globe for the kindergarten; organize after-school typing lessons; bring in jars of tadpoles; cart a busload of kids off to the Indian museum or to the nearest planetarium; bring in raw wool and dye it with dandelion juice; rig up a pulley system for the science corner; give lessons in creative writing; develop a file of community resource people or teach the kids how simple machines can turn eggs and flour into "Tagliatelle Harlequinata." Equally as important, they possess the human relations skills necessary to advise without insulting the professional educators. Don't ever fool yourself, the Worker Ants don't need the group at all; but without them, you would be just a bunch of rowdy dissidents.

2. Clearly establish the group's purpose. At the very first meeting, the die is cast. Is your group going to be an active, roll-up-your-sleeves-and-get-the-work-done organization or a forum for public wailing? Earlier, I mentioned the value in sharing parental concerns. Unfortunately, many groups quickly evolve into the single pursuit of this activity. I would suggest intermittent, but clearly social sessions for stories of past sieges and a direct, task-oriented approach to business meetings. Here's where leadership earns its good name. Elect a person capable of saying: "Yes, many of us have heard those cruel remarks from relatives; you were right to stand your ground. Now, did you volunteer for the Computer Capers or the Fun with Farina mini-class?"

3. Establish the group's structure. The specifics of organizing your group must depend upon need, resources and reason. Over-committee-ization has strangled many a cause. So keep the mechanism simple unless you really want to spend the rest of your adult life running a parent's group.

A few committees are essential. There are the:

- Watchdogs—to attend and take notes at all school board meetings. Your group must know what's going on to be meaningfully ongoing.
- Research & Development—to review the laws of your state, new trends in education, and gifted education in other school districts.
- Publicity—to gain membership and legitimize your organization. If you have a positive public image, you stand a better chance of being taken seriously.
- Activities—to establish enrichment classes, mentorships, field trips, family outings, scholarships, etc. These func-

tions should always be considered supplemental measures until the emergency passes. Unless you're prepared to start a new school, your goal should be to get the school system eventually to take over the details of GC education.

- Political—to support those school board members who actively favor gifted education and to bring about the replacement of those who do not. Don't be naïve about this. Aside from the few genuinely philanthropic souls, most school board members do it for power.

4. Learn all you can about the opposition. The most effectually disarming technique in any school's arsenal is, "We agree with what you're saying, but our budget can't cover that." School budgets are public documents of the school board. As such, they should be studied before confrontation. Find the accountants, lawyers and business managers in your parent group and form a financial review board.

5. Know what you want and be able to explain it to others. If possible, have evidence of how it worked somewhere else. I've seen intelligent, concerned GC parents approach a school board with lots of emotional gravy and very little meat. The fastest way of being dismissed as a histrionic is to come out with, "You've got to do something—our kids just aren't learning. I don't know what; but you've got to do it soon." Do your homework. If you avoid sounding like a know-it-all, but have sane, rational answers to the serious inquiries of the educators, you can become the community resource they turn to.

6. Prepare alternatives, time schedules, modifications, pilot plans, etc., for all your demands. Negotiation doesn't mean always getting everything you want the first time you ask for it. Nor does it mean that they'll expedite their promises without a watchful eye.

The most successful P.O.P. groups are those that can spot a hole in a school's curriculum and fill it with their own good-natured, diplomatically applied elbow grease.

WRONG: This is the most ridiculous, dumb-ass school system on the face of the planet. You people can't even come up with something meaningful for my genius to do. What the hell are you doing with our tax money?

BETTER: Mr. Principal, we've just discovered that the public library has access to 16 millimeter films of the PBS series "Nova." We'd be happy to provide volunteers to pick up and return the films for any of your teachers. If you like, we could put a note in the faculty lounge.

Some specifics that have worked for established P.O.P. groups:

- Build the school's science fair, spelling bee or theatrical production into a prestigious community event. After all, the whole town can turn out for a football game.
- Raise money for programmed instructional machines and software.
- Provide volunteer teachers' aides for enrichment classes, field trips and special interest clubs. (One father I know was nominated for sainthood after organizing, supervising and volunteering his office computer for a programming course.)
- Arrange a series of lectures from vocational role models.
- Establish a career day when members of your group take students to their offices, businesses, and job sites. (It takes planning and a cooperative boss, but unless you work in a high-risk or top-security area, it can usually be done.)
- Establish your school on the permanent routes of traveling media programs of regional museums, libraries, universities, etc.
- Construct a resource file of community people who can serve as mentors.
- Purchase resource materials for individual teachers or place materials in the faculty lounge.
- Provide guest speakers in the area of gifted education.
- Pay the tuition or fees for a teacher to attend classes, workshops, seminars, etc., on gifted education.

- Encourage the activism of the school's student government and clubs through study grants, resources, etc.
- Establish a parent library of educational materials in the lobby of your school.
- Raise money to buy something exciting for your first- or second-grade classrooms—a microscope or a dozen math game calculators.
- Establish a group of parents and teachers who will sweat through the grant application procedures for federal and private foundation monies.
- Organize a core of concerned, informed and highly verbal members to lobby for gifted education funds within your state legislature.

8. Plan for success. This means providing all the necessities of long-term committee management: in-service training for your old guard, orientation sessions for new members, long-term goals for gifted education in your community, welcome relief for all your Worker Ants, newsletters and other means of communication, provisions for the ego-saving admission of supportive educators and the involvement of the GCs themselves. (After all—it is their ballgame.)

IN A GROUP OR SOLO, YOU HAVE RIGHTS AS A PARENT

Many parents, because of their own school indoctrinations, feel very unsure as they question or threaten the competency of a school system. As an adult you might say, "They're the professionals—surely they know what's best." As a child, you (or your parents) may have said, "The teacher's always right."

Becoming actively involved with the details of your child's education can represent new frontiers for you. Your only experience with school may very well have been sitting in a class where the whole program was a mystery until the teacher told you what was important. ("Is this going to be on the test?") You may have caught on to the subliminal lesson: someone else had the answers. And now, here you are as a parent: daring to pose a different question, daring to doubt the teacher's word.

When the teachers and the principals and the school administrators and the counselors are right, they are also quite able (and often willing) to explain the details. And when they're wrong—well, that's why you've come to this party. So, your primal right as a parent is the right to ask the question.

You also have other, more specific (and in fact, legally and federally designated) rights:

1. You have the right to expect an appropriate all-inclusive education for your child.

2. You have a right to the written notice of any evaluations given your child. You have the right (though, believe me, you'll risk scorn) to attend such evaluations. You also have the right to attend teacher conferences in which your child and/or her test scores, school behavior, academic performance, etc., are being discussed with other teachers, counselors, and/or administrators.

3. You have the right to notification of any atypical educational placement (temporary and permanent) of your child and the right to appeal and periodically review that placement.

4. You have the right to submit an independent (professional) evaluation, be represented by counsel, cross-examine, present evidence, bring witnesses and receive a complete record of any conference, hearing or evaluation that will affect your child's educational placement.

5. You have the right to demand that your child be placed in the "least restrictive educational environment." This right is usually interpreted as applying to children with physical handicaps or mental retardation, but many experts in gifted education contend that the normal classroom is very restrictive for the GC.

6. You have the right to see your child's complete school record including test scores, teacher comments, formal disciplinary action, counselors' notes, etc. You have the right to copies. And you have the right to demand changes in the record that appear to be biased or incorrect.

If you've come this far into the book, I don't know what else I can say to motivate you to take an active and positive role in the special education of your GC.

To throw down the gauntlet: I could tell you that there will be plenty of us who will—and let you draw your own conclusions about the GCs left behind.

To pull at your heart: I could tell you one more horror tale of a GC whose talents were never realized.

Or to be honest: I could tell you that your kid deserves it. Besides, you're not a Gifted Parent if you don't.

Notes

1. Thomas A. Brodie, "Cooperation Among These Five School Boards Paid Off for Gifted Kids," *The American School Board Journal,* 167:2, February 1980.

Bibliography

Anastasi, Anne, *Psychological Testing.* The Macmillan Co.: New York, NY, 1976.

Bower, T. G. R., *A Primer of Infant Development.* W. H. Freeman & Co.: San Francisco, CA, 1977.

Buros, Oscar K., ed., *Mental Measurements Yearbook.* University of Nebraska Press: Lincoln, NE, 1972.

Buros, ed., *Tests in Print.* University of Nebraska Press: Lincoln, NE, 1974.

Delp, Jeanne L., and Ruth A. Martinson, *A Handbook for Parents of Gifted and Talented.* Ventura County Superintendent of Schools Office: Ventura, CA, 1977.

Fadely, Jack, and Virginia Hosler, *Understanding the Alpha Child at Home and School.* Charles C Thomas, Springfield, IL, 1979.

Gardner, Richard A., *Understanding Children.* Jason Aronson: New York, NY, 1973.

Ginsburg, Herbert, and Sylvia Opper, *Piaget's Theory of Intellectual Development: An Introduction.* Prentice-Hall: Englewood Cliffs, NJ, 1969.

Kamin, Leon J., *The Science and Politics of IQ.* Lawrence Erlbaum Assoc.: Potomac, MD, 1974.

Martinson, Ruth A., *Curriculum Enrichment for the Gifted in the Primary Grades.* Prentice-Hall: Englewood Cliffs, NJ, 1968.

Maynard, Fredelle, *Guiding Your Child to a More Creative Life.* Doubleday: New York, NY, 1973.

On Being Gifted. Mark Krueger, Project Director. Written by participants in the National Student Symposium on the Education of the Gifted and Talented. Sponsored by the American Association for Gifted Children. Walker & Co.: New York, NY, 1978.

Schaffer, Rudolph, *Mothering: The Developing Child Series.* Harvard University Press: Cambridge, MS, 1977.

Sharp, Evelyn, *The IQ Cult.* Coward, McCann & Geoghegan: New York, NY, 1972.

Stanley, Julian, ed., *The Gifted and the Creative: A Fifty-Year Perspective.* Johns Hopkins University Press: Baltimore, MD, 1977.

Torrance, E. Paul, *Gifted Child in the Classroom.* The Macmillan Co.: New York, NY, 1965.

Vail, Priscilla, *The World of the Gifted Child.* Walker & Co.: New York, NY, 1979.

White, Burton L., *The First Three Years of Life.* Prentice-Hall: Englewood Cliffs, NJ, 1975.

Index